This book is a must-read

❖ are interested in re

❖ want to discover h̶c̶ ......ts both those who serve and civilians trying to stay alive every day

❖ want to understand how people overcome adversity

❖ enjoy reading gritty memoirs

❖ want to explore what it takes to step out of your comfort zone

❖ need the inspiration to voice your own story

❖ want to grasp what a soldier's perspective of what the war in Ukraine is really like

❖ want to immerse yourself in a humanitarianism journey

❖ are trying to make a difference in the world around you

❖ are searching for your self-belief

❖ want to uncover the secrets of camaraderie and friendship.

"When I was asked to review this book, I was unaware of what it was about until I opened the pages.

As I started reading, Shareef's story started to unfold. Childhood experiences led him on his life journey to fulfil his desire as a military man to support the people of Ukraine. One starts to question whether his rationale was real or if was he battling against childhood challenges.

By the time I closed the book, it was very clear, whatever his reasoning, Shareef is a very brave man indeed. He knew what he was letting himself in for and engaged in warfare, training and supporting others in any way he could. Unless you have ever been there, despite the reports and newsreels, it is clearly a very different experience when you are right in it.

Shareef shares many insights into his life in Ukraine and of others living in a war zone. He shares the happy, funny, sad, fearful and traumatic moments. He earned the nickname Rambo after he survived his worst nightmare, from being seriously injured following a Russian attack. There was a risky journey back to the UK for urgent treatment. Even then he was reluctant to leave for it went against the odds of his values. I love that he included the personally written stories, of others who were pivotal on his journey.

I am full of admiration for a man that is not only kind, sincere and honourable, but brave in action and brave in sharing his story in his words. He helps the reader understand more about life as a military soldier and for the citizens of Ukraine. One can't but help take a moment to reflect and be grateful to all those like Shareef who are willing to risk their lives to fight for *Freedom at All Costs* for the people of Ukraine. I hope to meet Shareef one day and shake his hand."

Caroline Purvey
Author, Founder of TRE UK® and Creator of the unique Total Release Experience® Programme.

"As a veteran myself, I immediately recognised the spirit of adventure and inherent need to help people that leaps out from the pages of Shareef's book. Heroic and focused on an almost impossible mission, he thrust himself into the thick of a deeply hazardous environment to tackle tyranny and protect his fellow human beings. War is not what is portrayed in the movies, it is not glamorous; it is harrowing, and Shareef's story is a glaring reminder of those effects and dangers. Well done, Sir!"

Colin Tansley
Author, Veteran and Former Police Officer.

The views or opinions expressed in this book
are not attributable to the Ministry of Defence
or the British military services, but are strictly
the views and opinions of the author.

It reflects the author's present
recollections of experiences over time.
Some names and characteristics have been changed,
some events have been compressed,
and some dialogue has been recreated.

In addition, the text reflects the author's PTSD episodes
of reliving missions and experiences, so some of the
text is in the present tense to indicate this.

This book also contains past popular concepts. As a
consequence, some of the language is also reflective of
the times and is used to achieve context; such language
is not intended to be offensive, but rather to highlight
the general ignorance of the times.

RAMBO REEF

FREEDOM
AT ALL COSTS

A British Veteran's Experience
of the War in Ukraine

SHAREEF AMIN

First published in Great Britain in 2023
by Book Brilliance Publishing
265A Fir Tree Road, Epsom, Surrey, KT17 3LF
+44 (0)20 8641 5090
www.bookbrilliancepublishing.com
admin@bookbrilliancepublishing.com

A CIP catalogue record for this book is available
at the British Library.

ISBN 978-1-913770-63-1

To 'the Professor' Borodai Oleksandr Oleksandrovych who died defending *Freedom at All Costs.*

And to Shum (Oleh Shumov) who saved my life.

"…to the citizens of the world … come and fight side by side with the Ukrainians …

We are fighting … for our land...
And for our freedom…"

—President Volodymyr Zelensky

Contents

Foreword

When Vladimir Putin ordered his army to invade Ukraine on the morning of 24th February 2022 – beginning the largest and deadliest land war in Europe since the Second World War – he issued a stern warning.

Anyone deemed to be interfering with his so-called "special military operation" would face "consequences like you have never seen."

This threat, backed by 6,000 nuclear warheads, was designed to scare off Ukraine's Western allies and to break the will of Ukrainians to fight back. And Putin had good reason to believe it would work.

After all, the West had spent more than a decade turning a blind eye to Russian aggression the world over, fearful of escalating tensions with Russia. First in Chechnya, then in Georgia and Syria. Putin had already invaded Ukraine once, in 2014, and got away with little more than a slapped wrist.

Just six months before his second invasion, Mr Putin watched as America and its allies were chased out of

Afghanistan. The West, he believed, was in terminal decline. It would not, and could not, stand up for Ukraine.

Fortunately for us all, Putin was proved spectacularly wrong.

Ukraine, led by lion-hearted President Volodymyr Zelensky, resisted – dashing Russia's hopes of a quick victory and confounding experts who believed Kyiv would fall in just a few days.

The West resisted, sending unparalleled levels of military aid that now includes main battle tanks and may soon stretch to F-16 fighter jets.

And the world resisted, coming together at the UN to condemn the invasion with a near-unanimous vote that cowed even some of Russia's closest allies, like those in Beijing.

But the resistance of great men and global bodies would mean nothing at all if it were not for the resolve of the people at their back. The ordinary men and women, both in uniform and out of it, who heard history's call and decided to answer it.

Among them were 20,000 foreign volunteers who gave up the comfort and safety of home to travel to Ukraine and fight, putting their lives on the line in defence of a country and a people they likely knew little about – but whose cause they believed in.

Shareef Amin, a British Army veteran who had been part of the war in Afghanistan, was one of them. Determined to stop the spread of dictatorship in Europe, he flew to Ukraine almost as soon as the war began and taught them everything he knew. Then he took up arms with them, and almost paid the ultimate price.

Shelled and shot by Russian tanks and troops, he spent months recovering in Ukraine and the UK – time he used to pen this book – before returning to the front lines to serve once again evacuating casualties from battle.

His words now serve as their own warning to Putin: So long as people like Shareef exist with the courage to resist them, then their machinations will be doomed to failure.

His purpose and drive are unswerving – to fight for *Freedom at All Costs*.

· ·

Chris Pleasance

Freelance Global Affairs Reporter and ex-Chief Foreign Reporter at MailOnline
theworldexplained.co.uk

A Humanitarian's Purpose

TO PROTECT AND DEFEND AT ALL COSTS

When I arrived in Ukraine, my first job was to provide humanitarian aid wherever needed. I offered general support and some form of comfort, which led to providing medical care and teaching basic life-saving first aid. It is the ripple effect you create each time you introduce someone to new knowledge or skill; saving lives matters. Before I knew it, I had trained and prepared everyday Ukrainians with the military skills to save lives, including their own. After a time, I led these men and headed to the front line. Taking a risk and pushing myself to the front line was about life and death. I knew that protecting villages and evacuating civilians would save more lives, and the risk was worth it.

Let's not sugar-coat these situations. Every time you move forward, every bone in your body aches, every emotion felt, and every sense heightened. Every thought in your head is telling you to go the other way. It was the time for the mindset of a trained soldier and somebody who is a protector to come into play. Intense training teaches and prepares you to ignore fear. But when you're with your team, your Band of Brothers, that extra special bond infuses you with knowing that you're doing something to save lives; the pride and the honour inside your heart will not allow you to retreat. You have to keep going for your team. You have to keep going for yourself. War is a risky business that sacrifices lives for a significant cause, usually freedom. Although progress is with trepidation, you must believe you will return to fight another day. You think, "I hope it's not me." But you don't want it to be anyone else, either. However, you know full well that when you enter the conflict zone, it could be your last day.

WHY?

The intention of this story is not to impress with heroic actions, but to understand who you are and what it takes to lay down your life for a more significant cause than any individual.

When you consider all of our world's REAL heroes, they are ordinary men, women and children who have an incredible drive to take bold action and commit to and do extraordinary things.

It is not the Marvel, Hollywood or TV heroes who genuinely inspire you, for they live in a make-believe world of CGI, special effects and cinematography. They belong in your imagination and fantasies, yet particular human qualities will stir your emotions.

When you move to the REAL world, you can find the less glamorous heroes who walk among us daily. Consider the young man who jumps in the swirling river to save a drowning dog; the mother who runs into a burning building to rescue her child; the young person with cerebral palsy who walks a mile for someone less fortunate than themselves. These stories illustrate the indomitable human spirit that is in all of you. These inspired actions separate the extraordinary from the ordinary, showing you what is possible when you lean into something bigger than yourself. Whether it's saving a life, joining a cause or giving up everything to help people deal with uninvited struggle, you do something, and this is what making a difference in your life is all about.

Most often, it is not a conscious calling, but one that stirs your heart and soul and compels you to decide, choosing action over inertia, and going on the biggest and most rewarding adventure of your life.

This book charts a journey through adversity, not for pity or importance, but to show the strength of the human spirit, endeavour and for peace. The timeliness of this book is essential to gather momentum for the Liberation of Ukraine. I pledge to fight for freedom and for the Ukrainian people.

As human beings, we're born free. The idea of being forced into a particular way of life by a regime or tearing your life apart because of one selfish person's ideology is unacceptable. Murdered civilians and repressed families; in these untenable situations, no one can live their daily lives peacefully.

I've seen an inordinate amount of suffering, primarily through my military service. Even today, living within our free and peaceful United Kingdom, when I witness any racism, oppression and prejudice, it frustrates me. We're all human beings, and I feel these emotions strongly as an empath. Watching people suffering in Ukraine ignited my drive to take action. It triggered my thoughts of the consequences if they were left without hope and support from other peace-loving countries in the United Nations and Europe. I knew it was time to draw on all I had learned about life and what it takes to protect and defend victims of war. I had learned that opening your mind further strengthens the compelling need to do something. It is a force deep inside I call values that drive me to take risks, particularly 'freedom', which was the catalyst that propelled me into action.

Knowing that the Russian invasion could push through Ukraine and make it towards the Polish borders, increasing the chances of a third world war, was a significant part of my decision to help Ukrainians in any way I could. And I felt that it wasn't just Ukraine's war. It's our responsibility to stand up and do something against this type of dictatorship; if none of us takes a stance, inaction results and we cannot impact any change.

Subsequently, personally, emotionally and morally, I felt obligated to do something because I had the precise skills, mindset and drive to contribute. It would be worthwhile if I could help save one life.

Freedom is a human value that I honour with my body. It is the right of every man, woman and child, and I vow to use my life to protect this pillar of civilisation. Like all people, Ukrainians have a right to embrace their sovereignty and live in peace. Within these pages, you will learn about their indomitable spirit, as a David fighting a Goliath, who will never give up or trade their glory.

Struggle and fighting are no strangers to me. Even while I was putting this book together, I experienced immense challenges. Being gravely wounded, in excruciating pain and undergoing regular operations, not to mention my delicate mental health, lead to many communication issues and difficulties. As a determined human being, I had to find a solution to telling and sharing my story. In the end my publisher and I reverted to voice notes to commit these words to paper and share the suffering, brave endeavours and resilience of the Ukrainian people.

You always find a way when you have a mission bigger than yourself.

My name is Shareef Amin. I am a Humanitarian, Soldier and Protector, sharing stories of my journey to a place where I fight for *Freedom at All Costs* and, in the process, Find Freedom, Purpose and Meaning as a man.

Freedom

"To be free is not merely to cast off one's chains
but to live in a way that respects and enhances
the freedom of others."

—Nelson Mandela

What is Freedom?

As Japanologist Beth Kempton suggests, freedom is being willing and able to follow your life path as your authentic self. However, for many, the ideal of liberty eludes them, and they believe it is out of the reach of their grasp.

Like many abstract words, everyone will understand concepts, values and situations differently, depending on their experiences.

For many of us living in a first-world country, we can often take freedom for granted. The media floods our minds and senses with the overwhelming plights of people living with war, global change and hunger who

11

have no idea what it means to lead a life with freedom. Citizens of countries such as Syria, Myanmar and Somalia have limited freedom.

It is not only others who impact our freedom, it is often ourselves. I invite you to consider the stories and movies you play in your head. Beware of your thoughts, because you can easily imprison yourself with your self-talk. Consider the times you have told yourself you 'can't', called yourself hopeless or stupid, or questioned who you indeed are. These thoughts are monkey chatter and represent the tip of the iceberg of how you chat to yourself each day. Here is the scary part; when you listen, this chatter steals your freedom by preventing you from making good choices, doing what you want, or being who you are.

So, I ask you: Do you live your life with freedom?

Prologue

F uck, what just happened?

Where am I?

Is anyone there?

My mind did not know if it still belonged to me. Like a tsunami, thoughts and questions flooded my semi-conscious state. Confusion ran through my veins as I became more conscious of myself and the unfamiliar surroundings. Was I awakening from a deep sleep, or was I about to wake up from a living nightmare into another nightmarish world?

Why are my eyes not opening?

Why can't I feel my hands?

Why the fuck am I naked?

Most people welcome consciousness from a night's restful sleep, yet I am trying to remember and put together the pieces of what just happened. Piecing together the fragments was fruitless, as nothing was there.

The first face I saw was an angel. Her soft voice reassured me I was going to be okay. That statement in itself scared the hell out of me. *Why is she saying that to me? Why can't I remember anything?*

As my vision came into focus, I realised I lay in a hospital bed. *How did I get here?* Suddenly, the shock and realisation of what happened to me hit me like a brick wall. What the hell were all these tubes and wires oozing out of me from every orifice? Was I in some matrix? It was all too much. I tried to wriggle, yet nothing, no movement. Who was going to tell me what just happened?

The numbness wore off, only to be overtaken by searing pain, but I could not tell which part of me hurt the most. From head to toe felt like I had collided with a bus, and soon I would learn that it was not far from the truth.

I don't know how long I dipped in and out of consciousness. Was it the pain or lack of movement that jolted me into a recurring nightmare every time I opened my eyes?

What continued to haunt my mind were three questions:

What just happened?

How did I get here?

Why has my body been ravaged?

Like all good stories, let's start at the beginning…

PART I:
The Boy,
The Teenager,
The Man

Where It All Began...

Children love to run free in open spaces, and I was no different. I am sure you remember the feeling of the wind on your face. You feel alive and invigorated. The exhilaration and adrenaline run through your veins, and life at that moment feels good. It doesn't matter what else you are going through. My curiosity ignited bold action and risk; I know you understand this behaviour – experiences like these shape whom you become later in life.

I am the second of four children and life at home was dynamic and boisterous. My dad was a family-orientated man who had a pretty tumultuous relationship with my mum. My brother was always with my mum and two sisters, and I preferred to be around my dad. At the time, you do not consider how your relationship with your parents impacts you and paves the path to future relationships.

My mother is a loving, protective woman who has done much for me. She encouraged the bonding with my dad, and those unique but everyday moments have stuck massively in my heart and shaped my actions. Mothers are special people, and I am sure you can recall some special times and stories about your mother. Whether good or bad, she has shaped you into who you are today. As a deeply religious woman, she taught me about morals through my religious upbringing. Importantly, what has stuck with me is how to treat people and how not to treat them. That people-person development stemmed from her. It is often not until you are older that you consider your mother's significant impact on your life.

When it comes to graft and rolling your sleeves up, there was no more excellent role model for me than my dad. I had an unwritten bond with him. I favoured him when it came to family disputes, and when he wanted to go to the pub, I wanted to go with him. I loved being around my dad.

My dad was an aircraft engine engineer, and when the recession hit, that job dried up. He would go from job to job and I witnessed a man who never gave up. Providing for his family was his ultimate goal. If he wasn't making sales, he was designing kitchens, even though it was not his trained profession. He would use his engineering skills; he was resourceful like that. I particularly remember my dad buying and selling cars and fixing them to ensure that we had enough food. My dad took his responsibility seriously as a provider. He influenced my life and taught me to keep going, to never give up, and to be responsible for my actions.

My parents' relationship and the fact that they did not see eye to eye soon revealed itself, resulting in our family unit being somewhat dysfunctional. I would describe my parents' marriage as a 'little bit out there'. Despite that, my parents cared about my siblings and me, and the love and security we received in amongst the chaos have created a good foundation on which I can build my life.

I've discovered I love strong family bonds and values, which give you the confidence to take risks. No doubt your family dynamics and relationships growing up reflect different stories.

As part of a large family, there was never a dull moment, and finding time and space for myself was pretty challenging. Yet that challenge would impact my drive to focus on others through service.

The Power of Pets

I always remember having a dog when I was a child. The power of pets teaches us so much about ourselves and how to treat others.

I loved having dogs in the house. We had a cat, but my dad and brother had asthma, and we soon realised that they were allergic to cats so we had to get rid of it. It was a shame as my mum loved cats, but I suppose this teaches you that even when you are fond of something that is not good for you, you must learn to let it go.

Our first dog was a Jack Russell/Dachshund cross. We called her Kylie after Kylie Minogue back in the day! She would come on all the caravan holidays with us. She was fantastic. If you've ever had a dog, you will understand when I say she was part of the family. It was so funny as my brother and sisters would dress her up in baby clothes and take her for walks in pushchairs and prams when we lived in Bristol. Having Kylie was a real family bonding experience; however, I remember a few arguments over the dog too. I'm sure you have great memories of sibling adventures, including times when you didn't always see eye to eye. It's a part of family life and learning to negotiate what you want.

All the dogs would be on leashes except Kylie; she'd be out in the morning like a cat, so that was the nearest we had to owning a cat again! We loved that early morning walk around the whole neighbourhood. There is nothing like walking a dog, to help you discover your area and get to know your local streets. Being on a leash is restrictive; dogs, like children, need a sense of freedom to run around. Sometimes, when we let Kylie off the lead, she ran free as a bird. I swear, sometimes it looked like she was smiling. She was a delightful and loveable dog; we loved her to pieces. She reminded me how important it is to be free. I believe it was a significant value deep within me. Perhaps freedom is a driver for you.

And then we got a German Shepherd. He was a large, long-haired breed, and we named him Ben. It makes me chuckle; it was a very gentle name for a big dog! He was the softest dog and looked like a fluffy bear. Ben got on well with Kylie; it was like welcoming a new family member. Somehow he fitted right in, and we loved him despite him being so huge!

Humans and animals teach each other so much. When we respect each other, we find often the harmony that we are looking for. Have you ever owned a pet? Did it bond your family, or perhaps it had the opposite effect and caused a rift? Whatever your experience, it taught you about yourself and relationships.

Another positive aspect of having a dog was that it helped strengthen the bond between Dad and me. We were the ones who usually took Ben out for a walk. I remember particularly taking both dogs out on snowy days. It was great fun. We would find a bin lid or something we could use as a sledge, chuck the ball, and use the dogs as Huskies pulling us along. Ben loved it, and he would bolt through the snow like some crazed hound! Picture this substantial, powerful dog pulling kids along on the sledges! On other walks we would go to the park, when he would suddenly sprint ahead, with me holding on for dear life to his leash, my arm almost being pulled out of its socket whilst being dragged across the snow! Looking back at happy memories fills me with a sense of belonging and family. Life is often joyful when you look at things through the eyes of a child. I encourage you to do that as it's a great life tool.

As we go through childhood, our experiences shape the adults we become. I was a highly active, physical child, often outdoors or spending time with my father. Do you ever sit down and remember those far-off, carefree days? Sometimes you have to rely on a wild, childlike imagination, especially if, like me, you did not have anyone who inspired you to look beyond what you did in the moment or the next day to look to the future. Adults can be pretty busy, and I know it can make you feel like no one is on your side. Our insecurities growing up may skew the reality of the time. You do not understand such things as a kid, yet they still shape you.

Religion filled my childhood. My home and life had tight boundaries as we practised my mother's faith. She was a Jehovah's Witness, so as a child that was tough because we were not allowed to celebrate birthdays or Christmas. Can you imagine what that was like for a child at school? Perhaps you recall something that was at the heart of your upbringing? It is a challenge at the time and may impact what you choose to do in the future, but knowing this will provide you with some answers.

Putting Down Roots

Not only did I live with restrictive boundaries, but my family frequently moved around because of my father's job as an aircraft engineer.

Modern-day Bristol is one of those multicultural cities, despite its racist heritage. As a kid in the 1980s, I was oblivious to any racial tensions. My dad was Iraqi and my mother was white British, but I did not see myself as anything but British. No one tormented me, nor did I hear or see other evidence of racism at school. However, this 'free' living changed when we moved up North.

Around the age of eight, we moved from Bristol to the Midlands, to Kegworth near Leicester. We rarely had that settled feeling. How on earth was I supposed to put down roots, follow through on my curiosity, or explore my thoughts and emotions? I learnt at a young age to bottle them up. Being part of a relatively large family that moved around often raised issues for everyone.

My dad's job in Kegworth meant we were fortunate to live in a big, beautiful Victorian house with a great roaring fire. There was a huge field at the back where I spent lots of time with the dogs. We lived in a beautiful little village. Knowing we were staying near Sherwood Forest was exciting, and I grew to love the area.

We went to the local school. I became confused as I had not realised that the school was 'against' anyone new who lived outside of the area. At the time, Dad was doing well for himself and went to work in the town. He witnessed much racism for being an Arab. It was not long before it boiled over into my school life.

One situation imprinted in my brain living in Kegworth was that I experienced racism for the first time. I had never thought of who I was in terms of culture, race and upbringing, but I soon learned I was a 'mixed-race' kid. I remember explicitly going to school and trying to play football; it was a very unpleasant experience as the children were so mean and hurtful. On one occasion, I tried to shoot a goal and missed. The teacher laughed, as did all the other kids. That experience put me off playing football for an extremely long time.

Another time I asked the teacher to tie the shoelaces of my 'daps'. Most kids called them trainers. As I had called them daps, everyone laughed. After she loosely tied them, I fell and banged my head on the carpet. Again, everyone laughed. It became lonely because no one wanted to socialise or hang around with me at school. I don't think my younger brother experienced the same bias as me because he was in a younger class.

Childhood games can take on a sinister meaning without intention. A kid in my class was the subject of a vile game. It was like one of those 'tag' games. The other kids in the class would touch him and shout, "Vernon's disease!" They would continue the game by connecting with others and shouting, "Vernon's disease." It was as if they passed it on to whomever they touched. Things took a downturn when they started doing the same to me. I was now part of 'Vernon's disease'; I did not know kids could be so despicable.

At home, it was still unsettled: my dad was still struggling at work with racist attitudes. However, the straw that broke the camel's back was when the electrics failed. We spent a few months burning logs on the fire to keep warm. For some strange reason, this did not affect us much; it was the children at school talking about my skin colour that affected me far more. And that was the first time I realised that I was different.

As a ten-year-old boy, dealing with such chaos was part of everyday life and I did not know any different. Like all children, I accepted this way of living; it reflected who I am and where I belong, living up to my low expectations as a child and son. You have heard about the fight or flight mode when facing danger or challenges. Well, I was in that zone. As a family, we were dealing with all sorts of negative stuff, and it became too much. Sometimes you must cut your losses, try something new, know when to quit and move on.

As we tried to settle in Kegworth, I learned what racism meant. Similarly, as mentioned, my father experienced much unpleasantness at work. In the beginning, I didn't understand racism, so it didn't bother me; it was more about that feeling you get when adults belittle you and seem unmoved that you are being laughed at by the other kids. It leaves you singled out, which is a very lonely feeling. It fosters a sense of not belonging and worthlessness while not understanding why. It ignites a question of identity, something you take for granted as a child until challenged. You're unsure whether to question why you experience certain feelings and are often left confused. Life seems to speed up regarding how you view things, think differently, and suddenly have more questions than answers.

All of this left me not wanting to play football again because of something that the PE teacher had said about me. I didn't realise why I hated football so much until I started thinking about why. The outcome of these hurtful words was I sat on the sidelines after that event. I decided never to play football again. It was only later in life when I joined the Army that I got back into playing football but I was always in goal! Why do other people's destructive behaviours impact you so much? Why do some people shrug it off while others take it to heart, causing many mental health problems around self-esteem? It is crucial to question things and search for the answers. They are not always in the place you think.

It wasn't easy living in a different part of the UK. There is the notion of the North and South divide, and we experienced it at first hand. Other incidences occurred where I heard people say that they didn't want 'our kind' here – whatever that meant. It made my dad angry, and my mum struggled with it. The worsening situation was becoming too much for my mum, so she then stopped us from attending school. The tension at home was unbearable, so Mum left, returning to Bristol, leaving my brother and me with my dad up North. However, not long after she left, I returned to Bristol along with my dad and brother. My brother was missing my mum, and Dad was experiencing problems at work that had become untenable.

Once back in Bristol, everything seemed to settle again. We returned to the familiar territory we called home. After a short while, my dad had to consider finding another job, and there didn't seem to be the same amount of employment for an aircraft engineer anymore. It was a disheartening time as it seemed like we would have to start all over again.

Another memory that stands out in my childhood was play-fighting with my dad; it was just good father-and-son fun. My mum would always jump in and stop us from having what we considered an enjoyable father-and-son activity. I believe that play-fighting with your dad is a rite of passage, and it doesn't mean you develop violent tendencies.

As mentioned, my mum and dad sometimes didn't get on, and the family had a dysfunctional vibe. However, I recall my mum always being there for us. Yet it causes me confusion; was she controlling or caring? My mother was not a trusting woman, so she often believed my dad was in the pub, and sometimes he was and then again, sometimes he was making money so we could live comfortably. I often wondered why she wanted to think the worst of him.

As a child, my dad worked hard and spent all his time out of the house making money for us. I would often go to Blockbuster, a video rental store, along with all the other kids in the family. The film I remember taking out the most frequently was *The Sword in the Stone*. I can still picture the old building in the film that looks like a museum. My brother and sisters were fascinated by all of the action and magic in that film.

Sometimes Dad would wear his Arabian robe (the thawb), made from white linen with gold thread woven into it. On his head would be another piece of white material held in place with a black rope (a keffiyeh). It was a fantastic feeling when my father would put me under one arm of his robe and my sister under the other like a huge tent, and we would watch the film together with great happiness. It filled me with a sense of comfort and security. What I remember most is the smell of his aftershave; even now, confusingly, I am filled with sadness and joy when I think about it. They were great times watching the old VHS tapes, and it brought such happiness to watch my dad munching on a Crunchie while we chewed on fruit sweets, mainly Chewits and Fruit Pastilles!

The nineties reflected the usual childhood boy's stuff, like riding bikes, knocking on people's doors and running away, as well as playing football and on game consoles – typical ten-year-old stuff at the time. I remember going to the old quarry, swimming during the hot summer days to cool off and simply being daring amongst my friends. As young people, you unconsciously develop traits that will either support or hinder you as an adult. Taking risks is associated with an entrepreneurial mind, being a soldier, and science. Whether these risks are calculated or impulsive, they are always based on your conviction.

Game consoles were new then, but I preferred being outside and loved climbing trees, playing football and causing mischief. I remember when other boys played Cowboys and Indians; we ran around with sticks pretending we were soldiers at war. When you look back at what you did as a child, and who you were without limitations, you may find it reflects many aspects of who you are now as an adult. Considering what you did then and what you do now is an exciting exercise. You may not be doing what you want with your life, and you may still be trying to figure out your purpose. Looking back, the answer may lie in your childhood.

My dad was always there for me despite everything else that went on. I would take his side, no matter what. As kids, you don't understand all of the adult stuff around you, but my dad struggled and strived to make life as 'normal' as possible for us kids, especially in the late eighties and early nineties.

It is pretty intriguing how you can love both parents yet favour one.

As mentioned, your childhood shapes you, so perhaps my childhood story reveals some depths of my soul. You can try and understand how you responded to different people and events at the time. It is crucial to your mental health to pay attention to your experiences and not bury them, for they will come back to bite you later in life.

It's important to mention that at some time in life, everyone experiences prejudice. I see everyone as equal, so if I come across any form of racism, it has to be addressed; otherwise, it is as if I am condoning it. Despite the racism at school in Kegworth, I haven't suffered badly. And it's not something that has impacted me as much as others, as I have always seen myself as a white English man with brown skin. I just felt a bit of a misfit.

The Emerging Teenager

The whole experience of moving home, racism and being different left me feeling that I did not fit in with the crowd. I was constantly shaving my head and appearing like the cartoon character Tintin, with my trousers tucked inside my boots. I grew into a punk who loved heavy metal rock music. I seemed to drift. I wasn't the cool kid or the popular kid. I needed to find my identity.

As a young person, being accepted is everything. However, looking at those who stand out, there is a charisma and enigma about them. It takes courage, belief and a single-minded attitude to take action on what you feel inside as a young person. My experiences have encouraged others to stand out, even against the grain of community and society. Leaders do not fit in. They believe in themselves and stand out, and so must you if you are serious about making a difference in yourself, others and the world. As young people, the lack of experience and knowledge causes us to fall and we often make mistakes. But you know what they say about making mistakes? You learn from them!

My dad continued to influence my day-to-day thinking and started to impact the man I was becoming. We never spoke about my future or purpose – my dad was more like my friend, so we shared many moments but never had those deep conversations about what I would do with my life. Although aircraft engineer jobs were hard to come by due to the recession, it never stopped him from getting work. And he never gave up, whatever else was happening in the family. He would always be there to try and support us right up until the point when I left school.

I'm a bit hazy about what age I was when I began watching documentaries on TV and action movies, such as *Rocky* and *Total Recall*. For some strange reason, I was engrossed and drawn into war documentaries. Weirdly, it was not the fighting nor blood and gore that hooked me; instead, the people's plight, strife and struggle fascinated me. The adversity and fight against evil seemed to stir an intense feeling of injustice that struck me as unfair.

Remembering what type of books, music or TV/films you enjoyed and were fascinated by when growing up can help you figure out what is important to you. Looking back, I can see that my choices and experiences revealed who I was born to be: a compassionate humanitarian who wants to help others and make a difference. I was unafraid to fight for what was right, so my next decision and chapter revealed a new path. I always tell those who ask me about finding their purpose to try joining the dots in your past, especially as a child and young person; you will be surprised to uncover buried truths.

The Second World War was a complete enigma to my mind and way of thinking. The pictures often emblazoned into my mind felt like I was there, reliving the horrors of war. All I could think about was those people were trying to find their way in the world, but they had little or no choice. In front of them, they had the unimaginable force of the Third Reich. It was unbelievable to watch the Nazi party dominating Europe and beyond. But ordinary people with ordinary lives did extraordinary things during extraordinary times. They had a purpose, worth, and a goal that ultimately had to be achieved for the greater good of humanity.

Not only was I drawn into the fascinating world of war as a teenager, but I was intrigued by the politics of it. I wondered how one person could set off a chain of events that led back to them, and that everything they desired would fall into place for a significant world catastrophe. How could people allow it? This wave of propaganda and doctrine swept over them, and they spuriously were drawn into the charismatic leader's rhetoric and ideology like moths to a flame. It baffled me how an ordinary civilisation could even listen to one man's extremism and block out the outside world's reality.

I knew these people would have to rise and fight for what was right and overcome their struggles; it sticks in my mind and heart. I continued to watch these documentaries because there were lessons in their stories for us to sit up and notice. As a teenager, these documentaries filled me with a sense that I was born in the wrong era and time. At that stage, I didn't feel I had a purpose, yet there was something in the injustice and futility of war that would become my North Star.

As my school years were coming to an end at the age of fifteen, I started hanging around with the wrong crowd. We smoked weed, and school was never on my agenda; there was more playing truant than attending...

I would go to school and usually arrive late, only to be lined up against the wall with all the other latecomers and misfits. Of course, along with that came the usual bollocking from the PE teacher. One day, when he left us to go and get something, we decided to leave. My school had two outfields before the boundary. We legged it as fast as we could, with the teacher chasing us, yelling at us to stop, but we had youth on our side and soon outran him. Once past the boundary, there was nothing the school could do. Freedom was ours.

Being with 'my crowd' was far more appealing than going to school because they accepted me for who I was. I always felt out of place wherever I went, which is tough for a young man to process, with issues around my identity impacting my self-esteem.

Despite my challenges, one thing stirred deep within me; I had empathy for others. Even if I got into a fight when someone was an absolute bugger, immediately after punching them, I felt intense guilt. It did not matter even if I defended myself; the guilt engulfed me. Sometimes if I hit them too hard, I would feel their pain. Confusion rushed through my mind and body; it was an odd dilemma. I felt a definite dysfunction in my life. Teenage years can do that to you. I wanted to be an adult, yet I did not have the tools to cope with life's challenges.

When someone was in pain of any kind or upset, I was drawn to them as I had the compulsion to fix them. The intensity of feeling their emotion soon made me understand that I was an empath. There are always two sides to circumstances and personalities. I soon realised that by being me, I became a bit of a target, and because of my empathetic tendencies, people began to take advantage of my good nature. This sort of treatment by others is too difficult for a chaotic teenager's mind to figure out.

Looking back on my childhood, I cannot recall having that 'someone' who gave me direction, encouraged me to improve, and asked what I wanted to be when I grew up. The most prominent thing I remember is religion, religion, religion. Instead of shaping me as my mother believed it would, it caused great resentment, and I chose to run away from it. I moved out of the house when I was fifteen and went straight into work with my dad in the computer shop, helping him run it before venturing into the security world at twenty-one. For the best part of those five years, living by my own devices became the norm.

Becoming a Man

As a boy, I suppose you begin to think of yourself as a man when you leave school; that was when I was only fifteen.

At the time, I thought it wasn't so bad because I could spend more time with my hero and best friend – my dad. We started buying and selling the old-school Super Nintendo computer games (NES), which were the first Nintendo games consoles at car boot sales. We were good, and after about a year or so, my dad had saved enough money to open a small shop buying and selling games, virtual games and a few other things, including air rifles. Again, my dad raised and saved enough money through his success in the shop and managed to open another one. Who would believe that we would have two shops? I was so proud of my dad, and I know that witnessing his determination, work ethic and attitude of not giving up rubbed off on me. My father illustrated many significant life lessons of a positive role model, which gave me a sense of gratitude.

I began to see my dad differently. Perhaps it was because I was growing into a man, but I realised my dad was brilliant. He went from having no job with nothing, to a man who built not one but two shops, simply by buying and selling CDs, video games and air rifles. Pride buzzed through my veins.

One thing that created unease and frustration was the feeling of not being able to live up to Dad's achievements. However, I always strived to reflect on his drive, and it was fabulous to see it in action. Although we worked hard, we'd always have jokes and laughs, and sometimes we would still play-fight, and he would call it the 'pain zone'. Any time my mum was around, she would jump in, just like she did when I was a young boy because she's protective. Now that I viewed myself as a young man, I would tell her off for protecting me, and then my dad and I would carry on.

These are some of the highlights of my rite of passage into manhood, and they filled me with determination and strength, just like my dad, to pursue life making choices, whether right or wrong, usually deemed by the outside world.

However, one thing that struck me was that I had no direction; you could say I did not know my purpose in life. I was always searching for the missing piece. It felt like there was a hole, a space inside my chest. It seemed like no matter what I did, there was a perpetual hollow within me, and nothing I did filled it. There was a constant search to fulfil that void and I knew by helping people, it filled me with a sense of worth and meaning. Whatever I chose to do, it had to be something worthwhile.

As a young boy and teenager, you do not fully understand life's 'whats' and 'whys'.

Often your head is filled with what has been happening around you and within your family, community and society. You believe you must fall in love, find a career and be like your parents. Nothing seemed to focus on the individual, and no one asked me what I wanted out of life. There appeared to be an enormous expectation, yet at the same time, it felt like no one cared.

If values drive you, listen to your gut feeling and act on your instincts. The downside is that people may sometimes ask you to do something simply because you are a nice guy, and they see you as easy prey. I don't look for much in the way of repayment, but as humans, we like to be appreciated. I believe it is right to show gratitude and appreciation when others act kindly. When you come across someone with that 'nice guy mentality,' it can impact many aspects of your life, including relationships. Sometimes you must ask yourself, why you are that 'nice guy'. Is it because you want people to like you, or do you feel fulfilled by being 'nice', kind and empathetic towards others? The answer to these questions can also make a difference to your mental well-being.

When I worked with my dad as a teenager, I remember one poor guy always coming into the shop and asking to borrow money. Compassionately, Dad would always give him some cash for food. Sometimes my dad would know people's back stories and try to give them money. People can be proud, and a few would struggle to take it; he would ignore them and thrust the money into their hands. He had an intense drive, always needing to help somebody financially, even when it left him short. It was the same with the family; my dad would go without again if either me or my brother and sisters needed money. His personality and kindness highlighted his determination to ensure everyone else was okay. He never seemed to put his needs first.

Getting an education, finding a job and getting married did not appeal to me, yet the memories of those war documentaries etched in my mind were the seeds that, if nurtured and tended to, would lead me to a place that brought meaning to my life. Knowing who I was became vital for my peace of mind because I realised that I am different from everyone else. I don't understand things in the same way as others; I have both dyslexia and dyspraxia, neither of which was diagnosed when I was a child. I never learned in a typical classroom environment; I learnt through action and doing.

Leaving school and helping my father in his computer workshop provided the realisation that I was gathering computer knowledge through active learning. Working with my dad was a stop-gap. I recognised that the education system had let me down, given that they did not address my unique needs correctly, which could have shaped my motivation to learn and enabled me to thrive at a younger age. My disinterest in school and lack of education unfortunately now held me back from what I wanted to do. It hampered my drive in choosing to lead a purposeful life.

I have often asked myself why some cultures value education more than others. In the UK, every child has access to free education. One way to look at education is that it is lifelong. While most people use childhood education to achieve qualifications, it is possible today to achieve them at different times, stages and ages in your life.

In my twenties, we won a small amount of money on the lottery; it wasn't much, maybe a thousand pounds back in the late 1990s. My dad wanted to make more money with this opportunity, so we spent several days, perhaps a week or so, on a meagre budget, sourcing caravans, then bought as many as we could. I was so excited as I was allowed to go with him. We spent around a week sourcing paint and making steps for the caravans. It was one of the best weeks of my life, just my dad and me spending time painting the caravans and having a laugh and a joke.

After a long hard day, we would sit outside the pub in the sunshine, as inside it smelled of old beer and cigarette smoke. I remember him having a beer and cracking open one of those old glass Coca-Cola bottles. I would watch my dad, now and again, staring into his glass, wondering how and what we would do next. I can still smell the pub, him smoking a cigarette and having a Crunchie beside him. The vivid memory of us chatting, laughing and driving around in the car still leaves me with a warm, loving feeling. It was a great father and son bonding time; no limitations, just chatting and laughing. At this time, Dad brought up the subject of the Army. He had been in the Army himself, and planted a seed which gave rise to me considering life in the military.

We travelled around in the car and one day we went to a shop and, I don't know why, but I bought myself a marionette clown as it just intrigued me. I know it was a completely random thing to do, yet it filled me with joy and contentment. My dad and I sat and watched the sunset, and we would talk about nothing in particular, just simple father-son things. It was always a laugh. I watched my first sunset with my dad. An image imprinted in my mind forever.

When you are content in life or with a particular person who dramatically influences and impacts you, it can lead to impulsivity, and you find yourself doing strange things. One thing for sure is they will always stick with you throughout your life and be something significant.

It was not until I reached adulthood that I found something that began to make sense in my life, something that fulfilled my soul.

Me when I was about five years old.

A joyful picture of me with my dad, Laith, full of paternal love.

My dad, Laith, in traditional Arab robes (the thawb).

Me looking extremely smart at my passing out parade in the Army.

Who Are You?

Many people ask themselves, "Who am I?". Have you ever wondered who you are? Some people don't even entertain the idea because we tend to live outward-looking lives. When you ask this question, the usual answers include, "I am a father," "... a mother," "... a nurse," or "... an athlete." They focus on what they do, the labels with which societies define people. Others go a little further and respond with phrases like, "I enjoy swimming," "I love to cook for my family," and "I need to help people."

You could ask various questions to allow yourself to explore a different part of you and venture into a new world. Most people find it challenging to be honest with themselves. It takes immense courage to learn that the answer lies within yourself. It is about being brave enough to go on an inner journey to discover the real you, which is often hidden. The intention of this book is to take you on a journey through my eyes, embark on an adventure and discover who you are.

If someone asked you, "What are your values?" would you be able to answer them? What if they asked, "What do you stand for?"? Do you consciously know? It is equally important to know what you will not tolerate in life too. By answering these deep, thought-provoking questions, you begin to glimpse who you are.

Although I was not fully aware of living a value-led life, unconsciously I was so doing. Being aware that war influenced how I thought and felt about it because of its detrimental impact on human life, was carried with me from childhood into adulthood. I knew there was a bigger purpose for me as if I had an itch in the back of my head. No matter how much I scratched it, it was always there.

It wasn't until the 9/11 attacks that I took decisive action.

The Path of Destiny

11th September 2001 is a day I and millions of others will never forget. I distinctly remember being nineteen years old, up early in the morning, watching the news. I watched in disbelief as a plane struck the Twin Towers in New York City. I felt utterly shocked as the first plane crashed into the high-rise building. It was like watching an action movie. My first thought after the initial incident was that it had to be an accident. People's reactions were "Oh my God, is this for real?" Questions, incomprehension and shock were etched across people's faces. "How can a plane fly into a building by accident?"

Shortly after the first plane hit, a second plane hit the second tower. At the time, I think many people thought it was a TV replay of the first flight. But disbelief surged through everyone's veins as it was shown to be live on our TV screens. Even the news reporters looked stunned. What was this terrible disaster we were witnessing? It soon dawned on the world that not one but two planes had flown directly into the Twin Towers in New York City.

It was like living in a surreal world. My young mind struggled to take in and believe what I had just witnessed. I was in shock, my family and friends were in shock, the whole world was in shock and disbelief.

The reactions and flailing thoughts took a while to settle before I realised this was not a mistake or an accident, but a deliberate act of aggression. But who would do such a thing? Thoughts kept swirling around my mind; not one plane but two planes; not one building, but two buildings. Instantly, I was consumed by fear and believed it was the start of a third world war. America suffered an attack. Who would have thought someone would have the courage to carry out such atrocities? There were other attacks as well, such as the attack on the Pentagon and the attack on the capital Washington DC, which was foiled by passengers on board the flight. They lost their lives for freedom.

There had previously been a feeling of insane invincibility in America, that no one would ever touch them. No one would ever dare be so foolish. And in a flash, that certainty was gone – America was now vulnerable.

Hang on a minute, I thought, *this also means that the UK is not invincible.* We too are vulnerable to attack, and after watching the unfolding devastation in America, we're not all as safe as we thought we were. At the time, I didn't have much direction on what I wanted to do with my life. The closest thing I ever felt I wanted as a career was to become an animator or to go from job to job like an entrepreneur; that was my pipe dream. I knew I would love to work with my hands or design and create cartoons. Now, however, my mind was filled with finding a new sense of purpose.

I remember distinctly thinking "Wow!" as an intense fear in my heart shocked me into a sense of having to do *something*. Yet the reality hit me hard, as I felt I couldn't do anything. All I could focus on was what if this illusion of the spread of a third world war was to come home? I only knew what I had read and watched on TV about war. Would it be like the First and Second World Wars? Young impressionable minds swarm with 'what-ifs' and live with wild imaginations, and it felt like the world was just about to start another world war. A false sense of reality projected my thoughts towards worrying about my friends and family. Unanswered questions relating to the future fizzed in my brain – what was going to happen? These vivid thoughts hit me heavily.

Turning back to what just happened, I had a barrage of questions. *What is the death toll? What are the reasons behind it? How are the people on the planes feeling knowing what is about to happen? How are the people in the towers feeling as they try to flee the carnage? What are the people in the second tower thinking as they witness the first tower collapsing?* Mayhem fuelled with fear springs to mind. Terrible and unthinkable!

I felt useless. It hastened me into thinking about my life and what I had achieved. What could I do with my education and experiences to help and make a difference? It's a challenging exercise, but sometimes a huge life event gives you the opportunity to change your path.

The feelings aroused and forced me to think about what I would do with my life.

Despite my learning issues, having left school early, I had a burning desire to do something good in my life and felt that I had some purpose, but I did not yet know what that was.

One night after 9/11, my father and I discussed the potential of me joining the police force or the Army. I thought that if I wanted to join the police force, perhaps my inexperience in life would be a barrier. Maybe I would stand a better chance of joining the military, where I could do something worthwhile, get involved in whatever was going on in the world, gain knowledge and skills, and come out with new training and experiences. Surely joining the Army would be beneficial if I then decided to join the police? I intended to protect civilians, help people and do an excellent job.

Life has such a magical way of opening doors of opportunities, especially in adversity and desperate times. I finally ended up applying for the Army. It was a long-winded process as, being of Iraqi heritage, they had to do extra background checks. But eventually, I entered military life.

Joining the Army

No matter what happens to me, I have found my dad to be my biggest supporter. Like all parents, it can be a shock when their son proclaims he is signing up for military life. My mother was distraught when I left for the training camp. I can still remember seeing her at the front window by the curtain, waving me goodbye, and I could see the pain in her eyes.

I joined the infantry, and it was the first time I felt I belonged to something, a cause and a reason. I wasn't joining the Army to get a job; I signed up because the world was under attack, and I believed I could do something. The cherry on the top was that the Army accepted me despite my low educational grades, but focused more on my drive and fitness.

As you progress in the Army, you benefit from more in-depth training. It begins with Phase One training which means breaking down the civilian way of life. The focus is on improving your fitness and teaching you discipline, and this normally takes about fourteen weeks. In Phase Two, you can decide if you want to branch off into a trade or become a detailer, part of a small group created for a specific mission, and then you increase your knowledge of different weapons systems. This additional training enables you to become a professional using all sorts of weapons. Professional tactics involve doing exercises; these are war games. Phase Two is exceptionally intense and arduous, but you are considered a professional soldier once completed.

As part of my training and experiences, I gained considerable skills related to warfare, conflict zones and front lines. Initially, you know the talents are life-saving in that situation, but you don't always consider their universal importance in other cases. I was in deep training for two years and had to redo Phase Two three times for a variety of reasons. Over that time, I engaged in numerous activities and exercises. However, being well-trained in combat does not prepare you for when you leave the Army and join Civvy Street.

Afghanistan

I remember Family Day when recruits could invite their families to the army training grounds just before going to Afghanistan. Even though you don't know what you will face or experience in a war zone, instead of trying to persuade me to stay, my dad put my interests first and said, "Okay, if you are going away, we'll support you." All that mattered to my dad was that I should be happy.

Before long, I deployed to Afghanistan in Four Platoon – we gave ourselves the nickname of 'The Fighting Four'. Our call sign was COBRA 20. During this tour, the hearts and mind stuff began to set in, and I felt a sense of fulfilment being of service to the Afghan people. However, it was not until I went to Ukraine of my own volition that the actual depth of my purpose emerged. I had found the missing piece and the hole in my chest closed. I now believe that my humanitarian commitment to Ukraine is the reason I was born. The feeling of not belonging, the sense of no purpose and the feeling of searching for who I am as a man disappeared.

While I was in Afghanistan, we all received parcels from home. I think I only ever received packages from my father. It would contain sweets, letters and lots of other stuff that I liked and would be of use, such as toiletries. This generous gesture is significant in my life, as it shows my dad supported me and wanted to help me. It reminded me of all those times he helped people in trouble, especially with their finances.

At that time, the Afghan presence in Iraq was winding down. However, we were still concerned with terrorism and had an idea of where the Taliban were and that Al-Qaeda was known to be in the UK and hitting France, Germany and America. I was living with purpose, doing something good and feeling fulfilled. The Army's objective was to eliminate an oppressive regime that wanted to turn back time on a country that had already been through war and oppression. Furthermore, it seemed like they had declared war on anything Westernised. I took this personally as a Westerner, as were my friends, family and country.

Finally, I was doing a job that I felt passionate about, providing me with a purpose in life and identity which I craved. I wore a uniform with pride, which consequently endowed me with respect from my family and friends. Additionally, the pride in knowing I was protecting them and my homeland by going to Afghanistan motivated me to continue making a difference. Being a soldier defined me for a long time and, to some extent, still does.

Much of Afghanistan is still fresh in my mind. I remember our first patrol. It was hot, and I was patrolling the town as a new guy. One evening as the sun was going down, I distinctly recall hearing the call to prayer from the speakers on poles around the mud compound buildings and mosques. We were patrolling along the road where the guys in front of us were using the metal detectors called Vallons. It was a sweeping motion from left to right, in patrol position, which is staggered, where one man is to your left or slightly in front; you're somewhat to the right and behind him, and it zigzags behind. The reason behind this particular formation is to minimise casualties if any grenade is triggered. It is also protection in case you hit an IED.

I embraced all activity as I focused on being out in Afghanistan doing meaningful work. There were times when it felt like being on a film set, especially where you heard the call to prayer going on at the same time as you were minesweeping – quite surreal! I had to pinch myself because this was real; here I was, a guy with no direction from the UK, out in Afghanistan in a war zone. The first-class, tough training I had received in the British Army gave me the knowledge and skills that I needed to do the job in a professional manner.

The sound of shots brought me back to reality. These were not your usual shots fired in your direction; these shots were what they called shoot-and-scoot, where someone would fire from maybe 100 metres away in a hidden ditch. It is a rapid-fire sound, *op op op, op op op*. We had learnt to get into an extended line, fire back, and then roll the enemies by bounding forward and taking them, but we were dealing with different tactics in Afghanistan.

I had no experience of this situation, but you soon learn what to do.

Faced with a new situation, everyone hurriedly jumped into the irrigation ditches that flooded the fields. A few shots returned, and I still expected us to attack the enemy. Adrenaline was pumping through my body, the call to prayer was still going, and shots whizzed past our heads. They made a buzzing sound: *bzzwhish, bzzwhish, bzzwhish*. When something makes whishing sounds just above your head, and you hear a crack and snap, you know that you better keep your head down low. Strangely, I wasn't scared. You become desensitised to these adrenaline-induced situations in training. Slightly surprised, we waited to see if more shots would hail down on us. Convinced that the attack or warning was over, we jumped back onto the road and started patrolling again. Not long after, we arrived at our compound safe and sound.

What stays with me most about my tours in Afghanistan is that they were pretty intense, with lots of action and very, very hot, where you sometimes could barely breathe. Inhalation was challenging, especially in the hottest weather, even in the shade.

Another experience that greatly impacted me was when we were on a week's mission. We were supposed to take a compound so the engineers could build a bridge. However, whilst on the mission we were then given a three-day assignment. We took minimal kit, ammunition and water, as it was meant to be a short mission. We jumped into our Chinook helicopter and flew to our destination to discover that Four Platoon was the first to arrive.

Once we landed, we went into all-around defence, a complete 360-degree looking outwards position to ensure the helicopter was safe as it lifted off. Once in that position, no one leaves until the helicopter takes off. The wind from the helicopter hit hard as the Chinooks had recently received new Rolls-Royce engines. As a Chinook lifts off, you feel the immense heat from the back of these engines. And the gust of wind that comes up from the ground with all the gravel and sand will blow you about, no matter how much kit you carry to weigh you down.

It's a strange feeling as the Chinook flies off, leaving you in all-around defence in the sand and the sweltering heat that hits you while trying to stay as stable as possible. After the commotion, suddenly, you notice it is quieter, and you are left hearing the *chkoo, chkoo, chkoo* of the disappearing helicopter in the background, and then it's just silent. You sit there for a while, waiting to see if anyone will attack, and they don't… that's when you start to patrol the allocated area that is your responsibility.

Before long, it grew dark and, with our night vision goggles on, we fell back into a single-file formation. I was using the Vallon mine detector, sweeping our path to mark our safety.

Eventually, we arrived at a large compound. Our first action was to secure the area. We managed to set up in a small orchard where we spoke to one of the locals who reluctantly let us sleep there, although we were like sitting ducks as it was out in the open. We took up our sentry duties for that night in this vulnerable position. Thank God nothing happened.

We did the usual patrols to clear the area for the rest of the three days. The first patrol was in daylight, where we started to track down a road when, suddenly, all hell broke loose. We experienced machine gun fire and pot-shots being taken at us, so we started firing back. They would shoot at us and then scoot off. Because they weren't sustained attacks, we knew we were behind the enemy lines and wouldn't have an easy ride. Instinctively, we built sandbags along that route because it led up to the compound. It was arduous work as we did it all by hand up a hill.

We were putting the sandbags down and, now and then, bullets rained from across the river. Here we were, trying to build a defence with sandbag checkpoints, under fire. We endured the immense heat while trying to secure the area and do patrols which were far from easy; it was backbreaking work and very dangerous. However, as trained soldiers, we got on with it because we had to.

Another scenario while on this mission occurred again while we were patrolling. For the first time, we infiltrated a particular compound. By this time, we'd been out for about two weeks, and we'd only taken enough kit for three days as we believed it was only a short mission. We grew nervous – how long would our mission last?

A young lad from a different regiment had joined us at this stage. He had lost his night vision goggles, and decided to walk off independently without permission. He was then captured by the Taliban. The whole area was in lockdown – this is known as 'Man Away'. Later, one of our brother platoons found his body in a ditch. It was pretty gruesome, as the Taliban had executed him. We ended up being on that particular mission for six weeks.

We took over another farmer's compound and stayed there because we were looking to see where the Taliban's strong point was, as no one had ever been that far. When it was my turn for sentry duty, I was on top of one of the roofs when everyone was trying to settle. Out of nowhere, I saw rustling in the bushes. I had a friend on sentry duty at the machine gun, a general-purpose machine gun (GPMG).

I said, "Look over there, mate!" We thought it could be just a farmer. We couldn't just shoot anyone or attack anyone until ambushed first. Those were the rules of engagement.

Suddenly, out of nowhere, we hear the *thump, thump, thump*. Two rounds from underslung grenade launchers landed just in front of us, *boom, boom, boom*, maybe ten metres away from where we were! Thank God we were much higher up, so we started returning fire because it was the enemy, but we knew they would bug out (retreat rapidly) whilst dealing us another shoot-and-scoot.

The tension was mounting as we were extremely close. As my heart pounded, I realised the enemy was about thirty to forty metres away from us and in a flash, he disappeared. This situation was a stand-to (a state of readiness), and that's when we realised they weren't watching us but following us…

We stayed in the compound longer, but the order given was to bug out from there. So, we made it look like we had left. Even the enemy thought we had left, but we were hiding, waiting for a follow-up. When the locals came back in, we set up an ambush, but none of them had any weapons on them. However, we were sure that some of them were the people who'd attacked us because of the way they were dressed, but we couldn't do anything to prove it. We knew there were eyes on us at that point.

We decided to leave the compound and return to the previous compound we had initially secured. As we patrolled the area in a split formation across the fields, we became aware of a young teenager on a bike, on our left-hand side, following us. We gave him warning shots because we wondered what on earth he was doing. Was he reporting our location to the Taliban? We were crossing a lot of little bridges in many vulnerable areas. We continued patrolling and occasionally fired a couple of shots to warn him to back off, but he carried on following us.

The tension was growing. We moved into a village, and all the women and children disappeared. This was an ominous sign. The atmosphere suddenly changed and as we started to patrol the area, a battle kicked off. I am unsure how long it lasted, but eventually it died down, and the Taliban disappeared on their bikes.

It was time to leave here, so we found another area. As we entered the area, we found a command wire they had intended to pull and set off IEDs (improvised explosive devices) to kill us. Thankfully, we didn't set it off.

We called in the ISTAR EOD (explosive ordnance disposal) experts. The young teenager following us had indeed let the village know that we were turning up. As we waited in all-around defence, another ambush ensued. There was machine gun fire from behind us and machine gun fire to the left of us. We reacted to this as you do as trained soldiers. You put down fire, then the sergeant stops to give us orders. As we returned fire, we looked for muzzle flashes, movement and any indication of where the rounds were going.

Meanwhile, rounds were fast and furious, coming to the left and back of us. At the same time, the EOD team flew in by helicopter to deactivate the IED. There was action and tension all around. As they deactivated the IED, shooting started coming from the opposite direction from a wall about 100 metres to the left of us. The firefight had now been going on for a couple of hours. A few rounds whizzed past our heads, making a *whoosh, whoosh* sound; the sound was deafening as we could hear the EGL (Existing Ground Level) and rocket-propelled grenades (RPGs) going off.

During this action, I was in a muddy ditch with the machine gunner and a fellow soldier, Woody, who had the shotgun. We needed to get back to our platoon as we found ourselves divided. Unfortunately, two of the ISTAR guys who were deactivating the IEDs were injured, and my sergeant was dealing with two leg wounds and an arm wound. At the same time, we realised we were the target of machine gunfire and could hear shots from all directions.

Thankfully, we had one of our brother platoons join us for the fight. At this stage, it was encroaching on four hours of attack. We decided between us to push forward to reconnect with our platoon. At the same time, a helicopter was coming down to land to pick up the casualties. It was surreal, like something out of a movie. Everything was going on around us all at once. There was so much to take in.

As we stood up to break the treeline to move forward, I was the first man out, and as I broke contact, the enemy knew precisely our location. (A treeline is a line of trees that has been planted linearly rather than a natural feature of the landscape.) The whizzing grew louder as it passed above me. I could hear and feel *zoom, zoom, zoom* overhead.

As I pushed forward, we continued breaking the treeline but couldn't see the enemy. Worryingly, they had full coverage in front of us. I shouted to the boys back in the ditch that we couldn't see the enemy, but they could see us. I was now in the relative safety of the mud ditch, and we could see some muzzle flashes about 100 metres away from us. We began firing into and around where they were firing at us. We were trapped; we couldn't move forward, we couldn't move back. We were pinned down and had helicopters resounding above our heads.

We had RPGs going off and were about five hours into the battle. It was a full-blown war as far as the enemy was concerned. We finally decided that we needed to get ourselves out of this situation as we were rapidly running out of water and ammunition. People were getting hit, and we were losing coherency. The platoons were not moving forward, and we were not gaining ground. We needed to get out urgently, so we called our mortar team. A situation like this is called a 'danger close fire mission'.

We called in our top professional mortar team, who finally set fire. However, to start sending a fire mission, you must be about 300 metres away from the target before you can fire. We were only about 150 metres away and caught in the danger zone.

Suddenly, the most extensive firework display you can imagine ensued and hit these compounds. *Boom, boom, boom, boom, boom, boom,* from about six barrels and twelve nonstop rounds enveloped us. The ground rumbled and we could feel the air being sucked out and pushed back. We had to keep our heads down because we were so close to the action; remember, we were only 150 metres away. Bits of mud and gravel landed on our heads and all around us. The barrage lasted for what felt like forever but was only a few minutes, then everything died down. That was our cue to break cover again.

The helicopter took off back to base with casualties in tow, and silence now filled the air. Sadly, we never discovered if they arrived safely, and we will never know; the 'unknowing' is all part of the war. We didn't have time to check. We had to focus on moving back to the compound and keeping ourselves safe.

This was the first time I had that feeling of walking into a firefight – a battle using guns rather than bombs or other weapons – where your whole body is telling you not to move forward. However, your training overrides your sense of fight or flight, as you still have to push forward because you know you're doing it for your friends, your platoon and your section.

In addition, it is what you're trained to do. It is one of the reasons I was in Afghanistan in the first place; to fight for what I believed in and what I was doing. However, overriding that sense of fight or flight is an odd feeling as a soldier because you're doing everything against your instincts. The whole experience exemplified the training, need and necessity for survival. The first time will remain with you forever, but we had many more. The experience somehow makes it easier; you become more aware of what lies ahead and know how to deal with it better. The adrenaline is still there but is not as alien as your first experience.

I gave my best: I had set a goal, went out and achieved it. I did not excel, but I created opportunities to provide myself with experience and life skills, and even felt I had saved a few lives, yet I still didn't feel completely fulfilled.

PART II:
A COSSACK
FROM ENGLAND

A Cossack From England

My time as a soldier in Afghanistan taught me what it takes to be an effective team member in war and battle zones. As I reflected upon my time there, I began to focus on some life lessons learnt.

Military training prepares you for action and gives you the skills to deal with specific situations. However, it doesn't come close to doing the job in a war zone with everything else going on around you. You have practised the manoeuvres, handling and firing weapons, and it prepares you physically, but it is somewhat debatable that it prepares you mentally and emotionally for what you are about to face.

The practice field differs from the battlefield but gets you accustomed to the sounds of being shot at, the humanitarian side of things, dealing with the locals, and jumping from hearts and minds in one minute to fighting the next. One moment you are dealing with locals, and then in a flash you have to become a soldier and deal with aggression. It's difficult for most people to jump between those two extremes. But once you gain experience, it becomes a little easier.

During my time in Afghanistan, I would be on tour for seven months, sometimes longer; before I knew it, that became the norm. It is essential to adapt to your given environment at any point. You learn to change instantly, strengthening the flexibility of thinking and reaction. The training tries its best to support and prepare you for jumping from your regular day-to-day business to adopting the role of a soldier dealing with bombs and wounded people, and then flipping straight back into daily stuff, all in the blink of an eye. My experiences prepared me for a whole spectrum of emotions.

All the equipment I learned about and used in Afghanistan was identical in Ukraine. Most weapons are similar but have some nuances of difference, and you soon realise the variations. You learn about triggers, muzzles and safety catches. Once you know how to use a rifle, it's down to maintaining practice to keep sharp. You get five minutes to play around with them before using them in real-life war situations.

Within me, I still did not feel that total sense of freedom. As a member of the British Army, you are under the government banner, and restrictions prevent you from feeling truly free. After nine years of giving myself to the military, I have to admit I left in a negative state of mind. I thought I was not physically in a good place, so I felt bitterness towards the military, as I felt I had been left high and dry. My status as a single man with no kids was not a high enough priority to ensure I had all the requirements needed as I entered Civvy Street again. I felt rejected and asked why the Army was not looking after me. The road ahead looked long and dark. All these whirling thoughts impacted my perspective of the world and how I saw myself.

When I came out of the military, I didn't know what direction to take. I lost my identity and had no real aims or goals. Like many ex-military, I went through a few dead-end jobs and fell on hard times, resulting in depression. When we feel life has mistreated us, we often choose to go into a cycle of destruction. Many, like me, turn to drugs and alcohol to dampen the pain and the sense of hopelessness, with the perception that no one cares. I began to 'ruin' myself, attending many 'pity parties' but never feeling refreshed and renewed. Instead, I headed into the downward spiral of irresponsibility and pressed the repeat button.

Knowing that I give my all when I venture into something new, whether good or bad, I decided to focus on something more positive. At the same time, I was doing a night job and the lack of daylight was taking its toll. My way out of despair was to take responsibility for myself, so I hit the gym to get physically fit. My dedication to improving my physicality took me from a skinny lad to a well-built man.

As I was physically improving, I decided to get some qualifications with PSS (Paradigm Security Solutions), a close protection bodyguard company run by an ex-special forces guy named Rob Paxman. Rob is a former member of the SAS who also trains people to work in conflict zones. By choosing to work on myself, I soon got a job and had money in my pocket again, allowing me to get back on my feet. I liked this idea; venturing into this world again gave me direction and purpose. The benefit of working was that I started earning again! The protection industry attracts many ex-military. I had regained some fulfilment whilst I was doing this job.

You've always got that feeling of being a soldier that doesn't go away. Many guys end up married with families, but I was looking into joining the Territorial Army (TA) or reservists. Soldiering, protection and making a difference were in my blood and DNA. I was never satisfied and was always looking for something more.

In February 2022, Russia embarked on its 'special military operation' in Ukraine. This occasion seemed more violating than when Russia annexed Crimea in February 2014. For the last eight years, Ukrainians had lived knowing that it would only be a matter of time before Russia would shows its true colours and try to take over the entire country, obliterating its people, culture, history and sovereignty.

One day, I saw some images of Ukraine on the news. I will never forget one clip where an old guy stood outside his sandbagged house. He remained at his front door behind sandbags with an old-school rifle in his hands, waiting for the Russians to come through. Nothing and no one would stop him from living at home in peace. He was ready to fight for his right and freedom. Enraged, I knew these people were going to struggle. There in front of me was the might of the Russian bear against these poor people, ready to defend their sovereign rights and homeland. I knew then and there that I could help them in their hour of need.

I realised I was still not fully fulfilled in my bodyguard job. Now here was this opportunity to become a soldier again – perhaps more on my terms – and help a struggling country. Something inside me stirred when I heard the news, and an unwavering urge to get to Ukraine filled every cell in my body.

The childhood emotions that stirred within me when watching those Second World War documentaries years earlier went through my mind at a thousand miles per hour. And remember, my father had been in the military. The world seemed always in turmoil, and the war was never far from our TV screens on the news. Then 9/11 happened, which spurred me to join the military. The one thing that sticks in my mind about being a soldier is that it allows you to make a difference and feel fulfilled. I told myself a million times that if this situation happened today, I would be the first to jump into it and sign up to fight for my country and its freedom.

I could not believe this aggression was happening in Ukraine because of one man: Putin and his inhumane ideas. Between my night work and patrols, I was online, watching with disbelief at what was unfolding.

The next thing I knew, actions and stories were running through my head, and all I could hear was that inner voice saying, "You've got to get out there, Shareef"... but how do I get out there? I saw one guy on TikTok who managed to do it and questions ran amok in my mind. *Can I do the same?* I thought.

The instinct to go to Ukraine, offering hope to those civilians, and give them a fighting chance of winning, was intense and overpowering. The drive was compelling, so I wondered how easy it would be to go out to Ukraine, and these thoughts and images spurred me on. I researched how to get there and started investigating online forums and other sites.

I wanted to help the people of Ukraine. Without thinking straight, all that mattered was that I entered Ukraine, legally or illegally. I wanted to go over there to help the resistance. I knew I could help by showing them how to fire a rifle correctly, build up defences, or help in any way I could – even if just for a month, I knew it would make a difference. At that moment, it was more about supporting the people in whatever humanitarian way I could.

Sometimes in your life, you suddenly have a light bulb moment that you are here on this earth for a purpose. Most often, you do not understand it or even dare to believe it, but the haunting pull of doing something significant with your life is always in the back of your mind. Like my father, within me, there has always been a deep-rootedness to make a difference in people's lives, especially if you have the skill and know-how to do it. So when armed with all that information, how can you, as a human being, sit back and do nothing?

The realisation that my ambition to be a defender and protector revealed who I was, the **true** me. This purposeful role was my new calling. My British Army deployment in Afghanistan prepared me and provided me with the confidence, knowledge and skills to support Ukraine. I believed as a humanitarian and an ex-military man that I could be helpful to the civilians chosen to defend their country through conscription. The Cossack from England was ready to fight for *Freedom at All Costs*.

The green light came when the President of Ukraine, Volodymyr Zelensky, issued a call to arms of "friends of peace and democracy" to travel to Ukraine to fight against the illegal Russian invasion. His statement continued: "This is the beginning of a war against Europe, against European structures, against democracy, against basic human rights, against a global order of law, rules and peaceful coexistence."

This petition was a personal invitation from the President. Nothing could stop me now! I was pacing the room, shaking my head and chain-smoking. This conflict was my opportunity to do something great and fulfilling while helping to save lives. Committing to this action would make all the problems and struggles of my life worth it! Everything was building up to this moment. I knew it. I felt it in my blood. I made a decision.

I was glued to the TV as Zelensky encouraged people to imagine bombs landing in their communities and urged nations to apply more significant sanctions on Russia. He created a sense of urgency through his daily meetings with world leaders via video link, requesting as much support as they could give Ukraine, to halt the Russian advancement and bombardment. His straight-talking, heart-wrenching appeal made me more determined to go to Ukraine. Their sovereignty and freedom were at stake, and my sense of injustice would not allow me to remain inactive.

I am a man of action. More importantly, my morals and values begged me to question what kind of man I would be if I did nothing. There was only one answer. "Are you going to do this?" I repeated, "Are you going to do this?" Now was not the time to fall back on indecision; it was time to be decisive. "Do not go back on yourself. You need to get out there and do it! Fuck this, I'm doing it!"

In no time, I found myself online again, looking through different chat sites and asking how to get out there. I messaged one of the groups saying, "I'm going to Ukraine. Does anyone know how to get out there?" An American guy on a ship that was patrolling the oceans replied to me. He told me he could put me in touch with a group on WhatsApp called the Norman Brigade, a secretive combat unit fighting under Ukraine's flag, formed in 2022 by veterans from Canada, the United Kingdom and the United States.

Once I contacted them, they could not believe I would do it. You know that gulping sound you make when you step outside your comfort zone? Well, that was me and I made it. It was time to put my money where my mouth was.

There had been so much hype over the call that I could not even dare to think about backing out! I continued chatting with the Norman Brigade, and there was a considerable discussion, after which I discovered they were leaving in two days! My head felt scrambled. My initial thought was, *I can't go in two days; I can leave in a week. I don't get paid for another week and need some money.*

As the conversation continued, I had to think quickly, so I suggested we open another WhatsApp chat for Phase Two. Then we could syphon off the guys, such as myself, who could leave around the end of February/early March. Taking this action meant we could separate the information, what we could do immediately, and what the next stage would be.

Before I knew what was happening, twenty messages later, I received a statement saying, "I hear you are the commander of Norman Brigade Wave Two." I guess I had dared to ask questions, providing suggestions and solutions, showing signs of leadership.

I was stunned and had to compose myself quickly. Without another thought, I replied, "Am I? I guess I am, then." So this is how it feels to step up to the plate! The rest of the week threw my group into arranging body armour, equipment, flights and accommodation for the day we were to fly out.

"Is this the person I was born to be?" I asked myself. I am a professionally trained soldier, have been to a conflict zone previously and found myself in the best shape of my life. I was as ready as I would ever be. This person is me... Shareef Amin, finally doing something with a purpose that is meaningful for Ukrainians and me.

I am a soldier, a protector, and a man who loves to make a difference in people's lives, no matter what. It can be as small as driving an older person to an appointment, sharing a cup of tea, or chatting with another ex-veteran going through depression or anxiety. I describe myself as a Humanitarian. My sense of justice and love of people drive me to go beyond what I and others think is possible.

The human spirit can achieve anything it wants when you feel connected to a mission that is bigger than you. You begin to understand that you are a tiny cog in the wheel, but without you, progress lessens. When you view things this way, you realise that you are essential, that you matter, and you are needed by that more significant cause.

It takes time, effort and discussions to reach this understanding of life, but life takes on a new meaning when you do. It changes everything. Instead of dreading the day ahead and struggling to get out of bed, you have a new lease on life and feel invigorated knowing that you can make a difference in your life and the lives of others. You have a rush of energy that attracts other people to you, and the mission gives you a sense of fulfilment and that what you are doing for the betterment of life is essential.

Being a British veteran, I already had a Band of Brothers, so my initial idea was to reach out to them and share my mission. They didn't need much persuasion because being in the Army and of service is the seed that germinates a humanitarian spirit. This indomitable energy needs to find a purpose to grow and create positive change where needed.

This idea bore fruit in the formation of the ACS, a group of ex-servicemen led by myself – a Band of Brothers whose mission was to help Ukraine on the ground in any way they could.

Band of Brothers

Being part of a team is one of the most satisfying aspects of military life and projects. Working alongside people who share the same understanding, have a similar drive and want to make a difference adds meaning to your life at that time and in every moment. Having a team, meeting people and establishing lifelong friendships were my dream. Joining the Army and going on adventures are great experiences that are the basis for creating an authentic Band of Brothers. The excitement and unknown of getting to know each other, warts and all, is the culmination of coming together as a team, which is the foundation of being one unit under challenging situations and hardship.

On a superficial level, you can have friends, and they can be team members, and everything is bobbing along nicely and you all are having a great time. It isn't until things go wrong and difficult things happen within that team that you reveal the real essence of that person. In other words, you don't know who each other is or what each other's true colours and personalities are, until you have a shared hardship.

Being in a tight spot with someone, especially when you are on the front line, reveals traits such as determination, focus and the ability to work as a team. In these life-threatening situations, controlling your emotions is vital, which is challenging when you look death in the eye. With artillery, bullets and grenades going off in all directions, you need a cool head, and that's when all your training kicks in. It prepares you for autopilot actions and reactions because sometimes you do not even have the time to think. The drills we did in training prepare you for the battleground, but it is not until you experience it that you appreciate everything you have learned and the importance of teamwork.

Holding on to the outcome you envisage allows you to be positive in the face of adversity, and somehow you come out of it on a better side. Even when things don't go your way, you learn about each other and become stronger as a unit. It's about learning from the good and the bad, which is the secret of being a great soldier. The bonus of these shared experiences is that you become more robust as friends.

Like everything in life, there are two sides to the coin. Working and living in an intimate environment makes it easy to be attached to someone, but it doesn't mean you necessarily become strong and bonded. However, perspectives change when you go through hardships over long periods, particularly sharing pain, sorrow and life-changing struggles. The upside to this darkness which you experience is that you learn to be grateful and appreciate the good times even more.

When you put all these elements into a melting pot, it builds a Band of Brothers. There is a certain trust and knowledge of each person, and being acquainted with their mannerisms and different personalities shapes your tolerance. You can depend on each person to your left and right without worrying about what they will do next. Uncertainty has no place in a Band of Brothers. You build resilience knowing that you are safe in their hands, and they are safe in yours.

The whole concept of a Band of Brothers provides an identity and a sense of belonging. When you come to the end of your military career, it leaves an almighty chasm that is hard to fill. It is one of the significant reasons why soldiers miss the camaraderie and deep bonding when they leave the military, making them struggle in a typical day-to-day life. Most civilians do not have this closeness, this special bond.

On Civvy Street, you go to work, come home, have your dinner, drink with your mates, and have a laugh or a joke. If you get into a fight in the street, some guys may or may not help you. But when you have your Band of Brothers in the Army, you know they've got your back and will help you. Rather like the Three Musketeers, "One for all and all for one!"

The bond is established in those seriously strenuous training days when you get shouted at in your face and shot at when you're cold, soaking wet, miserable, tired and struggling. In addition, you are carrying a heavy weight, but you know you are not alone and everyone else is going through the same experiences. Problems like these provide opportunities to help each other, which continues into those challenging times when you are in the combat zones of war. You realise you are different because you must deal with blood, sweat and death while functioning both as a human and a unit. You take comfort in these times when you know you have a genuine Band of Brothers.

There is some comfort in knowing that you have some friends from the Army who still call you up ten or fifteen years down the line because that bond never goes away. Once a soldier, always a soldier; a deepened camaraderie connection is what we all strive for, and continue searching for. When you find it challenging to fill the void, I think it's one of the primary reasons many veterans, such as myself, return to war zones repeatedly because you meet the same type of people. There is such a human pull to be with like-minded people who make up your tribe, giving purpose and meaning to your life.

In Ukraine, we only wanted to work with like-minded soldiers or ex-soldiers in the long term because they have that fundamental Band of Brothers attitude and drive. This titanium-like bond is paramount to making progress and succeeding as a unit. It is the foundation of unity under challenging situations and hardships that would unfold in the coming months.

Arriving with the lads in Poland after our
journey from Bristol.

Some of the medics who helped me and my team.

Showing solidarity with Shum, who saved my life.

Even in the grip of war, it is important to take time to stop and appreciate nature in all its glory.

The wonderful Maria, one of the translators who decided to join us in the Band of Brothers.

In a field of sunflowers – the national flower
of Ukraine.

With a colleague,
making sure the
streets of the
town are safe for
ordinary people to
try and go about
their business.

Vikka, my brave and incredible translator.

In the trenches, getting some much-needed
shut-eye with a look-out.

A couple of my Band of Brothers.

All of the Brothers together.

In the midst of a war,
the perfect birthday cake.

Scan the QR code to
see my unforgettable
birthday surprise.

After a hard day's training, we still managed
somehow to find some beers!

Call of Duty

"It was a kind of siren song that called me out
to the front lines."

James Foley

J ames Foley was an American photojournalist who
covered the Syrian Civil War in 2012 and went to the
front lines to record horrific war stories in pictures. His
story resonates with me, reminding me of the age-old tale
of mermaids who lured fishermen to their deaths. The
magnetism of venturing to the front line was Foley's Call
of Duty.

However, he was captured and tortured for two years
before being brutally murdered by ISIS for his values
of moral courage, freedom and democracy. His legacy
continues with the James W. Foley Legacy Foundation, an
organisation set up to call for the freedom of all hostages
and to protect journalists and international travellers.
We remember him for his moral courage, photographic
war chronicles, and humanity.

Most men who fight for their country sign up as protectors, not to head for the front lines and kill other men. The nature of humans is to protect rather than kill, yet some men in history and today have no respect for human life, and they choose to destroy and kill. I consider soldiers as humanitarian, and this is how I describe myself.

Soldiers who put their lives on the line for others, their country or a cause, know that a human sacrifice is at stake; they hope and pray that it is not them.

Unless you live in a conflict zone or have survived the front line, it is challenging to know and understand its impact on the brave soldiers and people who choose to participate in that action as a Call of Duty. At best, we can show compassion, but empathy lies within the Band of Brothers.

Everyone who loves video games will know *Call of Duty*. I struggled with whether or not I should include this observation in such a serious, full-on, real-life narration. After some deliberation, I decided it was necessary to show two sides of the coin.

The game *Call of Duty* is the ultimate escapism, even though it tries to look and feel realistic. But it is the polar opposite of the horror and noise of being in the thick of a real-life battle, with your every move bringing consequences for you and those around you.

The citizens of Ukraine felt they had a Call of Duty to protect and defend their children, families, homes, villages and towns – and who could blame them? Indeed, would you not feel the same if your country was suddenly invaded illegally?

The real Call of Duty is NOT a game – it is a matter of life and death, where one is prepared to do whatever it takes for the sake of *Freedom at All Costs*.

PART III:
THE MISSION
IN UKRAINE

March 2022

Finally, it was the day we would all meet in person, 10th March 2022. We met at an old sailors' pub named The Hatchet in Bristol, a Grade II listed building dating back to 1606. We sat around a few tables, random men who had not met each other before, from all walks of life, all ex-military. There was general chit-chat as we drank a few pints, but now and then, we would look at each other, and that stare spoke volumes. We are all going to Ukraine; it was happening.

Amongst us were a medic, a sapper and a sniper. We had all different lengths of service, but we had that Band of Brothers as a common bond. A few guys never showed up, but that was okay too. We were here and would take on the mission to support Ukraine at all costs.

We didn't want to get completely plastered, so after a few pints, we left and went to the hostel, where we had reservations for the night.

We sat around for a while, continuing to chat about things in general. We each decided to sort out our kit and equipment. The medic took out the saline and tourniquets and shared the field dressings. He passed us our tourniquets. There was a real buzz in the air; I'd go as far as to say it was scary. *What is going to happen? Are we going to walk into a firefight without any weapons?* We had no idea what was going to greet us. Everyone was apprehensive but confident with our booked flights. The comradeship was evident as we were all checking that everyone had a suitable kit. Ensuring that we shared all the gear and equipment equally was important. Then it was time for bed: we were heading for Krakow in Poland first thing in the morning.

It was 11th March, and we had a plane to catch. Before I knew it, 16 of us were heading to Poland. I'm not going to lie to you, it was frightening, but the adrenaline rush of that trip fuelled the reality of embarking on a commitment that would change our lives.

We arrived at Bristol Airport to board the plane. The mission was on, and there was a bit of a buzz in the air powered by nervous energy.

When we finally landed in Poland, we intended to meet up with some other guys from around the country, but they didn't show. At the same time, there were a few guys in our group for whom the penny dropped, and they realised being in Ukraine was too much for them. We booked their tickets back to the UK because they didn't feel it was 'right' for them, or perhaps they lost their nerve. It's perfectly understandable; we were going into the unknown and had no idea what was lying ahead of us.

We had expected transport for the next part of our journey on arrival in Poland but soon discovered no vehicle was waiting as promised. This was frustrating and somewhat disheartening. People were meant to meet us, including SOCOM (Special Operations Command). Everyone was looking to me to make the decisions.

While trying to figure out the next move, we bumped into two random American guys who linked up with us. You could tell they were Americans because they wore a different camouflage uniform. We were joined by other nationalities – some Swedes, Finns and Romanians. There was no time to lose as we had to figure out how to get to Ukraine. Now, the real journey was about to begin.

We talked about our next step, seeing as we had been left in the lurch by the no-shows. *How on earth do we reach the border?* There was no information, no tour guide! Instinct and survival took hold, and we acted off the cuff. *Can we get a bus, train, or any type of vehicle? Where from?*

Finally, after much debate, we spoke to some taxi drivers who came to our aid. It was time to pool our money to pay for three cabs – remember, there were 16 of us and we all had a full kit. What a sight we were as we poured ourselves into the cabs! We were soon on our way down to the border of Poland and Ukraine.

The taxi drivers dropped us off, and we gathered our kit. The media was in full force, and humanitarian aid charities were everywhere you turned. It was chaos, absolute chaos. People were trying to shove cameras in our faces. "Who are you? Are you a foreign fighter?

Do you know what you are letting yourself in for?" Thankfully, someone came over and advised us to cover up our faces. Even though we were all carrying military kits, we had to walk as casually as possible. People were trying to ask us questions everywhere we turned, and we just refused to speak.

We finally found our way across the border. Some humanitarian aid employees directed us past tents and huts across the road. They were handing out water to refugees coming the other way. As far as the eye could see, cars were coming in and out across the border. There was much hustle and bustle as it was the beginning of a war, and an intense sense of nervousness hung in the air. Expectations were uncertain because we knew pro-Russians were among the crowds and we were foreigners. With no backing from our government, we were now under our own steam.

The line seemed not to be going anywhere as we stood in single file, close together – we were moving at a snail's pace. Once we finally got going, the experience taught us to stay in twos and threes as we walked through the huts and made our way to the border crossing. We realised we were lucky as this part was going more smoothly than expected. When we arrived at the border crossing, we handed over our passports and received kit and equipment. Now all checked, we were gestured onwards, and away we went…

Ukraine felt surreal at that point. We had no idea how to reach Lviv where we were supposed to meet some of my contacts. To add further tension, it was getting late.

Looking around us, we saw a group trying to book an English-Ukrainian get-together, so we started speaking to them. Eventually, we found the driver of a double-decker bus who pulled up next to us. One of the guards supervising the crowds beckoned the driver to where they were standing. We were super nervous because we didn't know whom the guard would speak to or where he would take us. Luckily, the driver opened the bus doors for us and we piled in. We had a double-decker bus to ourselves!

Our group now consisted of a Spanish guy, two Americans and about fourteen Brits, including myself. Our bus driver was a great guy and very friendly. As we were chatting, he revealed that there was a 10 p.m. curfew. Puzzled, with apprehension mounting, I had no idea what that meant. He explained that the police arrest you if you are on the streets after 10 p.m.

Keeping the panic at bay, I thought, *What do we do?* We had nowhere to stay, nowhere to sleep. We were about to breach a curfew with no accommodation and no contacts. Our predicament made me nervous, especially when I looked at the time. It was already 7.30 p.m., so we had two hours to find answers to all my tumbling thoughts. On top of that, the bus journey took about an hour.

When we finally arrived, it was dark. The bus terminated at the bus station and we said goodbye to the driver. At that time of night, we had no idea who was walking around. My over-imaginative and suspicious mind thought everyone was a spy or that someone would jump out and kidnap us. It was new territory, and everything was unfamiliar.

We decided to move into the bus station, an old concrete Soviet state building. Once we were inside the freezing grey building, there was hustle and bustle everywhere. Familiar smells from a hot dog stand, people hurrying to get in and out of the building, and the military driving up and down overwhelmed us; it all felt like a surreal scene from a movie.

After jolting ourselves back to reality, we realised we were all starving, so ordered some food from a small cafe and attempted to find out where we would go and what we would do. The clock was ticking… it was now 9 p.m. and we were only one hour away from curfew. A look of bewilderment washed over our faces: *What is going to happen?* I made some phone calls to a Brother from the Norman Brigade. Thankfully, shortly after, two vans turned up with some volunteers in the nick of time. There was a Canadian guy and some Ukrainian civilians too. It was 9.45 p.m. and we were finally in military care. They told us we were lucky because the curfew was about to begin. We had survived yet another hurdle – these guys were a godsend!

We threw our kits into the van and drove for about thirty minutes to what I can only describe as old university blocks, Soviet Union style. They stood block by block as far as you could see, but in and around these blocks were sandbags and trenches dug for air attacks. We followed a guy into the building and had our passports checked individually, including everything else we had brought with us. We were at the Georgian Legion headquarters, an ethnic Georgian military unit fighting with Ukraine who had made their HQ in these university buildings.

We walked into somewhere derelict, run-down, cold and wet, which reeked with a fusty old smell. The building we were occupying was an old music building, and it gave me the creeps. It felt incredibly spooky. There were accordions, tambourines and guitars strewn across the floor. People, including some militaries, were sprawled across the floor, lying on cardboard boxes and road maps. The sound of gasifier stoves going off and the hum of people chatting and trying to eat created a continuous noise which echoed in these old, once vacant buildings. There was no food, so thank God we had eaten before we arrived!

After settling in, I met Antony and Swampy, who looked after the British and American guys coming in to join the Legion. However, after being here for several days, we ran into a problem. Trying to establish ourselves and get our hands on some weapons proved extremely difficult. They refused to issue us with arms! They wanted to push us to the front line without weapons, and I was adamant that this would not happen. It was a battle of wills for a week or so with the Georgian commander, and we eventually ended in a stalemate. We'd set ourselves up trying to train the men and get our hands on some weapons, but he refused. After a few more air raids and growing frustration, some boys left.

In these confined, tense situations, rumours are rife. One story went around – and I didn't know how much truth was in it – that if you did not deploy to the Georgian Legion within the next 24 hours, they would shoot you in the back. Everyone, understandably, was filled with fear. Many of us didn't believe it, but as fear was there, it was our cue to get out. We had spent two and a half weeks in these buildings getting nowhere. It wasn't worth the wait; a massive air raid happened simultaneously, which helped us decide.

Then came the opportunity to skip out of line when the rest of the soldiers went downstairs. We dashed to the First World War-style trenches and used candles in the dark. Sirens were going off all around us. You can picture it; it was dark, with flashing lights, but we all stayed professional in our uniforms. Every man linked arms with the next man, and we would communicate down the line.

My mate Andrew and I made sure everyone was all right. Some of the guys stowed away in ambulances and took off back to the border, having decided that this was no longer for them due to the pressure they felt under, which is fair enough when you are knee-deep in a war zone. The rest of us waited for Harrison, a great guy and our connection man. He was the one that was organising everything for the humanitarian aid. He managed all the foreigners, putting them in strategic positions. A very resourceful man, he arranged two ambulances, another vehicle and a Sprinter minibus to get 'out of dodge'. Harrison's main concern was not to risk his boys getting shot in the back. And he realised we'd overstayed our welcome.

Some of the guys climbed into the ambulance. I jumped into a vehicle with a Ukrainian guy who spoke excellent English, and about fifteen guys clambered into the Sprinter with all of their kit and equipment. That was a squeeze and a push as we closed the doors behind them. About five or six guys were in the front, and about twelve were in the back, shoulder to shoulder. A rowdy crowd showed up at this critical point, so we all drove away quickly and safely towards another checkpoint.

We had no idea where we were going. Security men pulled us towards the right when we arrived at the first checkpoint. Always considering safety and security, I looked to the left and mumbled, *Please don't stop the Sprinter van.* I closed my eyes, and when I looked again, they pulled the men off to the side of the road, where they checked people's passports. All I could think about was, *Please let them through. Please, God, I hope they don't arrest them.* The next time I looked, all I could see was the Ukrainian guy praying. He was praying; he had pulled over and prayed for all of us; it was not a comforting sight.

I'm tentatively watching these coppers look around the van. They looked under it and checked passports. The thought was running through my mind like wildfire: *please don't open the back.* No sooner had I thought this, then one of the coppers went to the back of the Sprinter. He reached out and opened the doors... the look of bewilderment on his face on seeing twelve bulky foreign fighters standing, crammed shoulder to shoulder, like a tin of sardines, peering back at him, was a sight to behold. He said nothing, just laughed and shut the door. He slapped the van and sent it on its way. I breathed a sigh of relief and thought, the prayers had worked! We followed the Sprinter to another location, a halfway house, which turned out to be an unoccupied brothel…

After pulling outside the building, we squeezed about twenty guys into three small rooms. We settled in and waited for the mission's next stage, wondering what would happen afterwards.

We stayed here for three or four days, and it soon dawned on us that instead of sitting around doing nothing, we could always use some of the vehicles for humanitarian aid work, as we were not going home anytime soon. Harrison was the guy for the job, and he searched for a warehouse and soon found some assistance. About ten of us decided to jump on board and follow him. We split in half as some men wanted to push straight down to the front line to meet other guys. I wasn't sure about this decision and had to accept the halving of my team.

We next found ourselves in an old asylum next to a fire station. We settled in and we managed to buy the building. It took us a few days to purchase it through Harrison's funding. Feeling motivated, we organised the building and started filling it with medical aid. It was pure graft, and I loved it. Taking action always fires me up, and now I felt that I was doing something more purposeful. After all, this was why I had risked everything to come to Ukraine.

Before long, we started delivering aid from Lviv down to Odesa to an old school. It was destiny because we met an incredible woman named Vikka. She was a volunteer doing exceptional work for the hospitals. She would source medical supplies from wherever she could. Vikka seemed to know lots of different people and groups. She was a godsend who chose to support us. She was one of these people who could get you anything and put you in touch with the right people. Whatever you needed, Vikka had the answers.

The journey from Lviv to Odesa was eleven hours, and the Sprinter van and a couple of cars filled with aid didn't go fast. But we were doing something to help. It was a great feeling, and I felt like I was finally making a difference here.

When I first arrived in Odesa, the city's beauty struck me – the architecture, grand buildings, statues and gargoyles, cobbled streets and pure character. I've never seen a city like it.

One of the things that stood out for me was that there were some peculiar roads with confusing junctions, but when we first arrived, we noticed no cars on the road. There were barely any people there because they had all escaped the war. We saw the tram lines and thought they must be relics. We were fortunate to have a car to drive around in, and more importantly, we had a piece of paper with the all-important official blue stamp, allowing us to move and start navigating through the roadblocks. Without the blue authorisation, we would have got nowhere.

The train station in Odesa is grand and impressive. It is a beautiful city with great people, and I instantly fell in love with it. It was always my 'go back to' place whenever I wasn't on the front line. This was where we would return for rest and relaxation. Whenever we had some time out, we would visit the resort area. As you walked along the road, you wouldn't believe that the country was at war. It had a magic appeal in which you could lose yourself. To your right was the beautiful seaside with restaurants and bars; everything you could dream of for a relaxing holiday destination. There were even boat rides to take you away from reality's horrors and stress. However, the beaches, now mined and restricted, brought back the fact that we were in a conflict zone. But I felt it was the closest experience to 'normality' in a country at war.

Now and then, a rocket would go over your head, alerting you to the reality of war, even in a beautiful place. Notwithstanding the worrying situation, I met many new friends in Odesa, including Alex, Vikka's 'partner in crime'. It's where we set up home and stayed in our hostel whenever we needed a place to rest our weary heads. I find myself filled with deep emotion and a longing to return as I recollect these images and memories.

These are the same deep emotions that the people from Odesa felt as they returned to start their businesses during the summer when things were slightly more manageable. I was astonished to see the trams working. These colourful trams were a great character of the city and appeared from every direction. You could tell that they had been around the block a bit, as many were dented and tarnished. However, it was cheap to travel on them. I never used one personally because I had the car, but to see them floating around was amusing because it was hard to understand how they stuck to the roads with the bent and twisted rails. You soon learned to be aware so as not to be hit by them. Driving was crazy there as you had to avoid the trams and be alert about what was happening on the other side of the road. These trams were the king of the road, and more often than not, you didn't know whether or not they were coming.

I am eternally grateful to my friends and family who supported me financially in Ukraine. As mentioned, I worked a few months before leaving and saved up about £5,000. Some of the group used our money to support each other. Once you enter the zone, you learn to live frugally and have enough to cover your needs. Initially, we had received some funding to help with housing and living costs. But as the war became less prominent in the media, we received less and less funding. Gaining a contract on the front line became essential, as that would guarantee a pay cheque. Up until then, we were volunteers only.

We delivered sleeping bags for the troops, medical aid to the school and undertook food runs, but the long journeys and intense use of the vans resulted in many breakdowns. We ran the humanitarian assistance on handouts and relied on people's help for funding. We forgot the many challenges we had because the people at the school, who were distributing the aid to the troops on the front line, all expressed deep appreciation, which we sometimes found overwhelming.

I began believing this job was my calling and felt such joy. I experienced something new in this highly charged feel-good factor derived from tears of joy, hugs and people making friends. Vikka made our job easy as she seemed to know everything and was super-organised.

On one occasion, we went to the bank as we were broke and we needed money for a place to stay. For some mysterious reason, some helpers became very upset with us as we dropped off kit and equipment at the school. The women began screaming and shouting, telling us to get out. We soon learned that the rumours were going around that we were carrying weapons. Ironically, at this point, we weren't carrying any at all. The SBU (Security Service of Ukraine) came along and pulled their weapons out on us. They pinned us to the floor, repeatedly asking where the weapons were and asking to see our guns, but, of course, we had none. It was our first real scary moment as we had rifles and pistols held against our heads; they demanded our passports and also instructed us not to move.

This episode brought attention to the school, and Vikka, understandably, didn't like it at all. All our efforts over the last few weeks, building trust and relationships, went out the window. She didn't want us there anymore, so we decided to take our help elsewhere.

However, once an upset Vikka realised we told the truth, she broke away from the school and decided to join us.

She became our primary contact and helped us carry on doing our humanitarian work. We realised how vital Vikka would be for the next month as she opened our eyes to how critical Ukrainian women are in fighting the war. We learned at first hand what these unsung heroes do and how they try to support their men. This insight had a massive impact and provided me with a more focused drive to carry on supporting Ukraine in whatever way I could.

It was still only March! In these uncertain and unfamiliar times, we seemed to pack a lot of action and events into two or three weeks. Humans can achieve more than they realise when survival and focus feature in their every waking moment.

After the van fiasco with all of its breakdowns, we could no longer do these humanitarian and support runs to Odesa from Lviv until we could arrange and afford to have it fixed. Things were moving fast, and we urgently needed cheap accommodation after burning our bridges with the school.

As Vikka joined forces with us, she found a place called N1, a theatre transformed into a hospital. It was a quirky and strange place. Mannequin legs, tutus and masks were hanging on the walls, remnants of the theatre pre-invasion. There was a dance hall, stage mirrors and a bar, including secret underground bars and pubs. This impressive but bizarre building, with four storeys of small rooms, shared a huge reception area. In the middle of the room was a massive table, around which everyone socialised.

We met a guy called Sasha who owned the place. He was eccentric but a great guy who put the ten of us up, and we decided to stay there with Vikka until we decided on our next move.

At this point, we tried to get the vehicle fixed. Meanwhile, we thought about training some of the civilian population. We had previously spoken to Vikka about it and felt now was a good time to take action. She mentioned a group of guys and women who guarded the coastline across the bridge that could do with training on handling and operating a weapon. In other words, these guys needed some help defending their village. I agreed without hesitation, as this was one of the prime reason I came out to Ukraine, so I spoke to the boys. There were about six of us that wanted to get involved. Knowing I was making a difference and finally reusing the skills I learned as a British Army soldier was fantastic.

We came up with an arrangement. Vikka spoke to the border guards and the police, explaining the situation because we did not have the correct documents that would allow us to travel. We arranged a three-day meet and soon found ourselves heading down to an area where the group had gathered and started training with them.

As March came to a close, I knew I had made the right decision to travel to Ukraine. I met exceptional and brave people and, using my British military experience, began to protect and defend Ukrainians and join with them in fighting for *Freedom at All Costs*.

Me with the team, teaching citizens to defend their homes and their villages.

Teaching civilians how to fire and handle a rifle.

Important tactical training.

Training civilians on how to handle a stretcher.

Alison Thompson in the field, working with bandages.

Teaching manoeuvres to citizens.

Teaching civilians the tactics of war.

Transporting soldiers to the front line.

April 2022

We were so fortunate to have connected with Vikka. As our translator, she helped us with the language barrier and had excellent inside knowledge of the local communities. She was a great negotiator and supported us to help wherever possible with our big hearts and soldiering skills. I realised the simplest of acts could significantly impact a person's life. It is easy to take everything we know and do for granted. As a soldier, I learned how to handle and operate a gun expertly, and now as part of a Band of Brothers and army veterans, I was showing these life-saving skills to a group of civilians. It was an honour as people regarded us as highly trained soldiers out in Ukraine, compared to the reputations of most of the soldiers, which is why we ended up in the Special Forces. Putting your knowledge and skills to use in such circumstances adds a different meaning to your life.

Alex, Vikka's 'partner in crime', is a chef and a great guy. He always cooked food for us and couldn't do enough to help, including providing supplies, advising us where to go, and so on. Another friend, Paul, also lived in Odesa. You couldn't help but have a sense of sadness when marvelling at the Odesa Passage, a beautiful monumental hotel building representing the golden era of the city, a time of prosperity and stability. No matter where you turned, you saw jaw-dropping structures such as the impressive silver-grey turrets of the Holy Assumption Cathedral, which houses magnificent art and decorations. It is a prime example of the devotion of the people who come to pray.

My heart broke for these people and their city. Yet, they were hopeful, as their resilience and determination kept them going and fighting for their right to freedom was the only option.

On 2nd April, we decided to head to the village where a group of guys and girls had set up dormitories. Even though I hadn't planned a training programme, I thought, *It's only three days, so I'll resort to my old-school military training. I will present the basics of marksmanship principles: how to operate a weapon safely, defend the village, stop an attack and carry out some medical training.*

I could sleep easy knowing I had crafted a plan. When I awoke in the morning, I discovered I was the last to get up and go outside. But then I heard some singing – everyone was singing Happy Birthday to me! I was stunned as I had forgotten it was my 40th birthday! They had baked me a cake, and what was more surprising was that the whole village had turned up for me! All I could see were these glowing candles on the cake. Wow! Who would have thought it possible? It was the first time I had experienced a party like this, and it took me risking my life and coming to Ukraine to share this celebration. I will remember that day for the rest of my life!

Although thankful for this act of kindness, we soon found ourselves again in training. During the training, we went through lessons in the classroom, where everyone sat eager to learn. Step by step, I talked about my military training and had assistance from a few of the other guys in the group. I took the lead on this exercise while Vikka was the interpreter. Having her as part of our group was a blessing because she was our chief communicator, enabling us to teach these brave men and women.

The next stage of the training focused on the physical side of things: how to operate the weapons safely, where to not aim them and how to clean a rifle. These people needed to know how to shoot a gun or rifle and all the other effective tactics and actions that would keep them safe. The training lasted into the evening, when we started to consider tactical strategies.

I was impressed by the way these civilians took on the tasks. I had never seen anything like it. Learning these drills takes over six to eight months in the British military. They picked it up in hours because they had no choice as the threat was on their doorstep and coastline. You could see the Russian warships from our position. It was a long, tiring day of training, but truly worthwhile.

When we finished the training, out popped a candle and they started singing Happy Birthday again out of the blue. Next, they brought out some Borscht, a local

Ukrainian dish. It's a red soup made from fresh beetroots, beef shank, onions, carrots, potatoes, cabbage and dill, topped with a dollop of sour cream. It was delicious and superb, and I had never had it before. Talk about taking on new experiences and overcoming challenges! At the time, there was a curfew on alcohol, so these resourceful people were brewing their own alcoholic beverages. We downed a few drinks and had a great time.

Experiencing my landmark birthday in Ukraine solidified my love for these people and their country. It gave me the determination to keep going and intensified my desire to help them. The Ukrainians appreciated everything we were doing. I had my internal dialogue and feelings that I was there to help, and it seemed like no great feat to carry out. It was life or death for them; I could go home anytime, but they were stuck in war-torn Ukraine, defending their families and homes.

After a good night of drinking and lots of fun, we headed to our dormitories as we knew that the morning would bring more tough training. The next day, we went into medical training, learning how to use a tourniquet and first field dressings (FFD). It is a life-saving technique, so if, God forbid, any of them were to get injured, it would buy them time to get to the nearest hospital. This pivotal training started the training programme for the medical people and aid runs.

After the second training day, the civilians became aware of attacks on several of their villages. One of our Ukrainian friends had already experienced the fighting in his city. In addition, he helped Vikka with organising training programmes and training areas for civilians. Unfortunately, on a particular day, we had to cut short the training because of the seriousness of the situation. Some people had to check on their families, and we would help. It was an extremely worrying time.

Vikka, myself and another person were driving back from one of the checks. While Vikka was preoccupied with driving, I looked over and up to the right and saw people on the side of the road, looking up to the skies. It was then that I saw a trail of smoke. I became alarmed when I realised it had taken a right turn towards the direction of our vehicle. We were driving along at approximately 60 mph when I noticed a rocket trailing alongside us. Whilst I didn't think we were the target, it was worrying.

I turned to Vikka and said in broken English, "Vikka rocket! Vikka, rocket!" She was not paying attention, so I gave her a massive nudge, "Vikka, look to your left," just before turning back to see where the two red rockets were now. At this point, she put her foot down. About half a kilometre away from us and to our left, all we see and hear is *BOOM! BOOM! BOOM!*

It was a bit of a wake-up call. We did not need any more signs that the war was severe.

We continued the drive back to the N1 theatre hostel, settled down with our kits, took notes and debriefed with the team. During our stay at N1, we arranged more medical training activities and ended up having visitors coming to the hostel. During this time, I met Dr Alison Thompson, who founded Third Wave, and is involved in rescue work in war-torn countries. (You can read her story later in the book.) We became good friends and decided to join forces.

My team went to other areas to help supply the mobile hospitals with medical aid and training for the medical assistants. We were there, providing security for Alison and her nurses. We were involved in helping teach medical aspects of war injuries, such as how to stop bleeding using a tourniquet, how to bandage a head wound and how to deal with shrapnel wounds.

During this time, we would bounce around from A to B, in and around Odesa and other places in Ukraine, to train people to save lives. Alison would come and go every ten days with different nurses. The team and I would stay occupied by day-to-day activities and organising other training opportunities while trying to live a little. We cooked, and we had the chance here and there to have the odd beer and make plans. Simultaneously, we remained armed because the rocket attacks were becoming more frequent.

After finishing our official training days, we would return to our hostel to clean and freshen ourselves up. As mentioned, the theatre had a bar downstairs, which would feed and water the local defence forces, police and soldiers patrolling the areas, because there was a curfew at 6 p.m. in this area. I made a point of deliberately talking to the police and military, who were dubious about us initially, to the point that they raided us more than once. Sometimes, they would come to the hostel with rifles and hold them to our heads as they asked to see our passports three times. Eventually, they became used to us and were quite friendly.

After these experiences, we became aware that to be armed with weapons to defend ourselves and others, we would have to be contracted with the Ukrainian military to participate, continue and train. As April was coming to an end, we decided that we would approach the Army and explore options of how we could support them and at the same time, become armed and officially contracted, giving us credence to train. However, we did not want to go straight into the front line, as we intended to continue our humanitarian activities and the training of conscripted civilians as soldiers in preparation for the front line. We would stand shoulder to shoulder with the Ukrainians and fight for *Freedom at All Costs*.

Signing the contract to join the Special Forces.

As the humanitarian, supporting the work of
Alison and her team.

Alison delivering much-needed supplies to those
trapped in their homes.

Alison's van and some of the crew.

A poignant moment when the elderly take comfort from the support of Alison and her team.

Give us this day our daily bread – Alison ready to hand out provisions.

The joy on a babushka's face as she receives
her food parcel is worth everything that I
have been through.

Much-need
tinned provisions
for soldiers and
volunteers.

Alison amongst
the crucial
supplies for the
bombed-out
towns and villages.

Vital ration packs
needed when on
missions.

May 2022

As we entered the month of May, we continued with our mission to obtain arms and be contracted by the Army, which would improve our position and ability to move around village to village more freely.

At our hostel, we noticed some unusual activities involving the shop on the opposite side of the road. Our hostel had a little landing where we could smoke and use the small bar to watch what was happening in the street. We often saw two men standing outside the shop opposite, looking like they were grouting bricks. We became suspicious after a few days. I thought perhaps I was being paranoid, seeing these guys walking up and down the same street daily.

I mentioned it to the team, and they kept an eye on things. We kept the doors locked and were extra vigilant as part of our security strategies. Wherever we went, we were in groups of twos and fours and always spread across the road, taking turns to watch out in case anyone was following us. We would close the door behind us, making sure that someone would wait there for a while.

People would try to come in and say they wanted to use the hostel when we had booked it up completely. A couple of weeks later, we heard on the news about the arrest of ten spies within a kilometre of where we were staying in our street. One of them was a high-ranking official, so our suspicions were correct, and we knew we were being watched from then on.

We approached a brigade, part of the Ukrainian Defence Force; I mentioned who we were and our intentions. After all, my journey began when President Zelensky appealed to foreigners to come and help fight for democratic freedom, opened the doors and requested people from around the world to support the war. Confident in our abilities and military background to help the Ukrainians defend the city, we met with the commander and a couple of high-ranking officers to discuss our plans to support them with humanitarian aid and any training we could provide to protect Ukraine. The contracts drawn up indicated we would be flexible but on the condition that we would start training their troops, their conscripts. It was a big ask, but we had already shown that we could do it with civilians, so why not the troops?

The commander turned to us and said, "You have twenty-four hours tomorrow to train thirty men." Without hesitation, I said yes to his request. He relented a little and gave us ten days to train the troops, but this was still a big ask!

I arrived back at the hostel, spoke to the team, and considered what we needed. We had a whiteboard and nothing else, so we took a deep breath and off we went.

It was pretty daunting at the start. We went out the next day and assessed the area. We drove about two hours through the training area, a small village. There were a few cottages and grass as far as you could see. It looked like time had stood still there. A few carts, donkeys, cows and cattle were on the roads, and then the 'troops'.

The first thing to do was to assess them; they were conscripts. They were bakers, farmers and shop owners; they weren't soldiers! So we knew we had a mountain to climb. Here we were with six months' worth of NATO training to explain, and the commander wanted it carried out within ten days! These guys pushed us to the limit – I was shocked and told him that it was a nearly impossible task. The response? That victory was the only outcome. All we could do was push forward onto the next stage as best we could.

I referred back to my training with the British military, pulling out the key points. Thankfully, we had Vikka as our interpreter. We were a team of five, addressing about eighty men, instead of the thirty we had expected, which was crazy! Before we knew it, forty more men came along, and we ended up with 120 men… Under pressure, it is evident that our military training kicked in as we only had ten days to train them in tactical manoeuvres, patrols, shooting, marksmanship principles, defence and medical. You name it, we had to do it. It was time to step into overdrive.

I stood up in front of the classroom and introduced myself and the rest of the team. When we started the training, it was difficult at first because of the language barrier. Despite this hurdle, the eagerness of the men in front of us to learn was phenomenal. I've never seen a group soak up so much information so quickly. It brings to mind the saying, "Where there's a will, there's a way".

After the process, I found that everyone took on roles. I became the lead instructor as well as the drill sergeant. Rousing them to "move, move, move," if they messed up was highly effective. It was about instilling discipline in them – that trained soldier experience and our military approach gave them a much-needed uplift. Maintaining praise kept them going. Watching them progress from civilians to functioning as a team of soldiers was inspiring.

At the end of ten days, instead of being led by us and told what to do, how to attack, and how to defend, they were doing it alone. This positive response was a brilliantly rewarding experience, watching them transform from keen but untrained civilians, to trained, disciplined soldiers. They had a lot of information to take on board from trainers speaking a foreign language. But they managed it, and later on I was on the front line with some of them. Sadly, some of them didn't make it back.

Sometimes you have to pinch yourself because you can outdo your perceived limitations in the most adverse situations. We were winging it without a complete programme but had great courage, experience and expertise. When you have some self-belief as well as a more significant cause than you, it's incredible what you can achieve. I know because we did it with our programme during those arduous ten days.

Such was the level of our success that we had more requests to do the same again. However, this time, it seemed more manageable because we had more of an idea of what we were doing. Our confidence had improved so much that we could train civilians to go into live fire, and we had them moving and firing past each other exceptionally competently. Our success soon reached the commander and his team, delighted with our work. We were now in a great position to request and sign contracts, and become part of the Defence Force.

At the end of every training, I would give a debrief, talk to the troops and show them great appreciation to get their spirits up and re-energise them. They loved it, and I loved it; it was the day's highlight. We shouted, "Slava Ukraini!"(Glory to Ukraine!) and that last little bit was such a bonding experience. The team and I would then return to N1 to eat, chill out, listen to music or dance, and have drinks. I would sit downstairs with the owner, Sasha, and some of his friends. A couple of times, we'd have military music and sit around chatting in the hall or sometimes dancing on the small stage – it was a charming and relaxed atmosphere; quite surreal!

During April and May, 1 was finding my feet, learning new things with my friends at the start of the trip and the new friends I had made as I travelled around Ukraine. I was highly optimistic, and it was a full time in my life as I realised destiny was right before my eyes here and now – helping people in Ukraine in their hour of need. These new friends, some of whom I met briefly, many of whom I am still talking to today, made me fall in love with the people of Ukraine and solidified where I was supposed to be. I was being who I was meant to be, doing what I loved, protecting and defending democracy for *Freedom at All Costs*.

June / July 2022

June and July merge into one as the concept of time completely disappeared.

In the briefing with the commander, he intimated that we would be able to join the Defence Force. This contract started around early June. We ended up pushing down to the front line with 126 Territorial Defence units. We travelled to the front line in a convoy of six vehicles. These were not your usual military vehicles but civilian vehicles, which made the whole experience surreal. As we sped down the road, the indicators flashed and the traffic stopped for us. We were running red lights, which seemed the norm and felt exciting. Eventually, we veered away from the safety of the main roads, heading off-road towards the front line.

As we trundled along the dusty terrain, we saw once bustling villages and towns now decimated and ruined, and we realised that we were in the thick of a crazy and unnecessary war. We were driving like the clappers along a tree-lined section of the countryside. It was summertime and the spinning tyres were kicking up dust. We daren't go slowly because the Ukrainians had learned from previous experiences that Russians were known to appear out of nowhere and suddenly target any convoy. No one said anything, but we all felt the adrenaline pumping around our bodies. Luckily, nothing happened at this point.

We finally arrived at our destination, a village where its people held the front line. It was relatively small, with a little road and a factory at the end of it. The commander turned to us and said, "Right, here's your house." We were amazed – it was a small cottage-style bungalow with a driveway. In the village, there was a butcher and a garage. The instruction was to stay here and hold the line and that they would supply us with some weapons. They gave us some food and left us to our own devices.

We had to make this tiny house our home. We were building the defence and digging in. We filled sandbags, ensuring the windows were secure, and then set up our bed spaces in this tiny building. Each person makes their own little 'nest' where they can get comfortable. I was next to a window on the floor with my sleeping bag, and all my kit and equipment hung up on nails hammered into a wall. It was important for our safety to ensure that our kit and equipment were always tidy and ready, especially if we needed a quick exit. We were waiting on permission from the commander, all of us on tenterhooks, just holding the line.

It was a time of hypervigilance as we were expecting something to happen. The only thing that went on throughout the day was the temporary fire and mortar. We were in the middle of it. We would hear our mortars and artillery go over the top of our heads every day. The noise sounds like circular motions, whizzing, whirring and whistling. And you can tell which is yours because you hear a thunderous bang and a whoosh over the top of your head. When it comes from the other direction, you begin to worry. You know the enemy aims for your artillery, and the mortars set up somewhere behind you. The accuracy of these artillery mortars is pretty random.

Sometimes, the rounds and mortars would land in and around the house. It was a time of hope and prayer as we could do nothing about it. This situation continued for about two weeks until we realised that we wouldn't be assigned any mission other than to sit there and wait for something to happen. It was untenable; being sitting ducks was not what we signed up for. So we decided to leave as we weren't an artillery or mortar team but an infantry team. The instruction had been to sit there, waiting and watching, but we realised we wouldn't get any significant missions if we stayed there, waiting for the hit.

Being unable to utilise our military skills or experience fuelled our frustration and I felt it was detrimental to the Ukrainian defence. We had fulfilled our side of the bargain to train the troops, and then they put us in a unit where we became obsolete, and there was nothing we could do. We were there 'just in case' a tank might come along. We were almost like security for them, but this was not what we signed up for, so we spoke to the brigade commander and told him that the situation was not suitable for us. We had signed up for front line work;

we were an infantry unit, a specialised unit, trained to be on the move, be strategic and defend.

We stuck to our guns by cementing our decision that our skills and resources remain unused for our benefit, for Ukrainian civilians, or those of the military. Consequently, we requested removal from the area. It was time to reassess our situation and request deployment for more effectiveness; at this point, the brigade commander agreed and finally pulled us out. Without wasting any more time, we drove back to Lviv.

One of our team members decided to leave and do his own thing, which put a spanner in the works. He left without saying goodbye and took some unlawful equipment. We asked ourselves, "What are we going to do from here? What's our next move? What are we going to do now?" There was a lot of confusion, doubt and frustration.

After some deliberation, we decided to train troops until our next step, which revealed a new position. This decision allowed us to take some much-needed downtime back in Odesa and restore some balance in our lives – a little time for us. Here we could regroup and rethink.

We were in a great, beautiful city, so why not discover what it had to offer as a place to live? Now was the prime time to look around, as from since we had arrived in Ukraine, we had managed very little rest. It had been relentless humanitarian aid work, training troops, training medical staff. We had been doing everything we could, working with the Third Wave, supporting Alison as security and helping her with the medical training. We felt we needed a rest and regrouped, and with everyone in agreement, we took the necessary time out. We took about two weeks off to rest and recuperate, but the mindset of a soldier is always at the forefront of your thoughts, so we still managed to train a couple of troops!

On one occasion, I booked a high-rise apartment at a resort front. These apartments were expensive as no one wanted them because of the bomb attacks. It made it easy to rent one for a short break. I remember one of those days when a friend and I were enjoying relaxation, having a beer, when I decided to look outside. All I could hear was *dada, dada, dada,* and to my trained soldier's ear, I knew it was anti-air machine gun fire.

As I looked up to the sky, all I could see were trails. *Where are they heading?* I wondered. About two kilometres away, I could catch splashes. I counted one, two, three, four, five splashes and a plume of smoke. Small mushroom clouds formed, and smoke soon enveloped the city.

The strikes were not just on industrial targets but civilians. Huge bombs were exploding, and massive rockets were striking the heart of the city. I headed down in that direction because it was in and around the area meant to train the troops. I found this whole scenario quite shocking. To see the Russians hitting the city was senseless. I've seen rockets go off many times before, but to see them from a high-rise and watch them go from start to finish, knowing there were people down there being attacked, was terrible and appalling.

As a soldier, I knew this attack was not warfare but a war crime. They were explicitly and purposefully targeting civilians; those people were not military. It was not an army complex. I felt rage rush through my veins; every inch of me pulsated with disbelief and frustration as a human being to witness this atrocity at first hand.

By now, relaxation was the furthest thing from my mind. All that was going through my mind was that we, as foreigners, can fall back off the front line, but these people still have to deal with this war on their doorstep daily, as part of their everyday life. It makes you realise that even when you get a little bit comfortable and relaxed, there's a war still going on right here. It brought home the reason I was in Ukraine in the first place – and how important it was to carry on and get to the front line.

We waited for more contracts and learnt to be patient, biding our time. Ukraine has so much bureaucracy that it adds more time to the process. If it doesn't have a stamp on it, it's not official. Everything must have that blue stamp.

Meanwhile, as we were checking out the contracts, we felt that the news and interest in the war fizzled out, especially back in the UK, as much of the funding we received stopped. Consequently, we were scraping by, living with no money or help from anyone. However, we still had rent to pay and hoped the contracts would come sooner rather than later.

The month of June was frustrating – it felt like nothing was happening. We waited two months for the contracts to finally arrive, and there's only so much training you can do before you understand that moving forward is vital to your satisfaction.

At last, we received word about moving to the front line. Five of us were uncontracted, yet we jumped at the chance. We said, "Let's do this!" We wanted to push forward and leave the remaining guys behind to continue the humanitarian work. After all, we had prepared ourselves mentally and physically for several months for this very moment.

As June and July continued to roll into one, the days were hard to count and were about survival, protection and action.

When not contracted by Special Forces or anyone else, I often found myself attached to non-official missions. As Special Reconnaissance, we sneaked around, trying to get behind enemy lines, so there are no official records, only accounts by myself and others in my platoon.

It's a mixed feeling when the realisation hits you that you are on the front line. You are excited because all the training finally comes into play, yet you are apprehensive and unfamiliar with what lies ahead. Being with a group of guys you have already bonded with is a bonus because you have each other and an established camaraderie that exhibits an understanding of each other and the situation you are facing together.

The instruction was to head to the front line with weaponry from RPGs, Bell grenades, underslung grenade launchers (UGLs), machine guns, rifles and pistols. As well as the usual weaponry, we were fortunate to have some highly technical pieces of kit, such as a Javelin, one of the more effective weapons on battlefields across Ukraine, which targets armoured vehicles. We also had NLAWS (Next Generation Light Ant-Tank Weapon) – known as the "ultimate tank killer". We were utterly loaded, ready for missions.

On this mission, there were five of us officially attached to the Ukrainian military. Before we began our journey, we set ourselves up to prepare for our mission ahead which I knew would be fraught with danger, as we would be driving to the location of the front line.

Finally, we received the signal to move. Preparation is paramount; you must be ready to act once you receive the nod. Now that you feel the adrenaline pumping through your veins, your training makes the move flow easily and, more importantly, swiftly. We all jumped into the 4 x 4 to take us to the front line. Our team was fortunate and grateful as the vehicle had been bought through a friend, and part of our job initially had been to get it in complete working order.

We were driven across the country at high speeds, over bumps, snaking from side to side. The downside to adopting such high rates was that it kicked up tons of dust, obscuring visibility and making it doubly dangerous for the driver. However, it also kept us safe despite the circumstances, as we were almost hidden by the dust, speeding along these open grounds behind an artillery line of Russians. At the same time, explosions were going off in every direction as the Russians tried to hit and destroy the environment around us. Everything was happening at lightning speed; it was very rapid, like a roller coaster ride or a scene from an action movie. The vehicle was jumping in the air as we went over bumps and potholes; it was kind of crazy, with all the kit and equipment rattling and being thrown about from side to side.

Of course, we were all on tenterhooks, trying to make sure that nothing happened to the equipment as it was our only defence against the Russians, and the guys on the front line were depending on its safe arrival, ready for battle.

All in all, it was pretty exciting. I had to constantly remind myself that I was in the middle of an actual conflict zone, and this was no *Call of Duty* video game. We tried to go along with the ride until we hit the main hardstanding, riddled with potholes and ditches. The roads were strewn with evidence that the Russians had pushed up before us. All around, we could see the destruction of the old Russian positions. There were huge, massive craters; we could sense and feel the urgency for the retreat of the Russians to their strongholds.

I am not sure how long the journey took us, but we were glad when we finally arrived at the treeline as it would offer us some cover and shelter. We jumped out with all our kit and equipment into the treeline as quickly as we could, just in case the drones saw us. We had to be vigilant about what was all around us.

We fell into our patrol and set up positions with the Ukrainians, facing outwards towards the Russians.

We could see the Russian tanks and their locations approximately a couple of kilometres away. We noticed it looked like a fortified compound with observation points (OP).

Darkness descended, and we joined two other Ukrainian teams to patrol under the cover of darkness in an irrigation ditch so we were low to the ground. We were patrolling in single file, ensuring we kept ten yards apart, towards a specifically identified area, when a tank pulled up, shooting in our direction. It continued to tease and threaten us as it remained in one place for a while, and now and then would pull back, trying to lure us into a false sense of security.

The mission aimed to put down mines and anti-tank lines, but it was easy for the Russians to spot us, so we had to venture out during darkness for added cover. The focus was to move quickly and accurately while carrying lots of equipment. It's not easy running at pace with 30 kg on your back. Ahead of us were the anti-tank and mine guys, and we were at the back to cover them; we were their protection.

There's undoubtedly trust required when patrolling. You have to read body language and the silence. It was labour intensive as we were following the Ukrainian lead. Added pounds are put on your legs as you push through the long grass. During these times, you understand the reason for the punishing physical training you endured as a recruit. We were almost thankful for them, as without that prior experience, it would have been even more brutal than it was.

Memories flood your mind of the weaving tactics you practised in training as you dodge the potholes in concrete divots and try to stay within the dead ground (hidden ground due to the shape of the terrain). Now and then, we would get a light source from the enemy that illuminated the ground with its sulphur light, providing a vision for them to commence sporadic fire in your direction. Every time a light rose, our defence was to dive to the ground, heart pumping.

The darkness seemed to intensify the sound of a few machine gun fires in the background – *bah bah bah bah* – and we all hoped and prayed it wasn't going to be one of us. We knew they were close but had to hold on to the belief that they hadn't quite seen us. Perhaps they just spotted some movement, unsure whether it was an animal or the enemy. Like us, their adrenaline must have been pumping, and in the night, your eyes and mind play tricks on you, so they too must have been spooked. We would wait for the Shamoolies to die out, then wait for another couple of minutes, and then we'd be back on our feet. Then as if nothing had happened, we would carry on with the patrol.

These attacks happened often, and thankfully they missed us, but they were close enough for us to be tentative about our next move. We knew they had seen us, so we waited a bit longer. My mind was going into overdrive, scrambling with thoughts about my mortality. However, they did not send out tanks or a quick reaction force to seek and destroy us.

We now assumed that we were safe and continued patrolling up to our position, where we set up all-around defence and waited for the Ukrainian sappers to go forward.

These sappers should take twenty to thirty minutes to put down ten mines. They went forward, but it was too risky to do all ten, so they managed to get about six down, and within ten minutes, they bugged out, coming out the other way. We counted them in rapid succession, "One, two, three, four, five," before the final Ukrainian said, "Last man!" and that's when we knew it was time to move.

Mission accomplished safely; it was time for a fast patrol back to our original positions, where we remained for the night.

In the morning, we retreated to camp, which was a relief, especially knowing that we had all experienced a successful mission with no one killed or injured. This result strengthened the mindset of the whole group.

Sometime later, we learned that the tank we had encountered was damaged and probably destroyed by the Russians. It was their strategy to eliminate any proof that they had attacked us.

As we pushed towards the front line, we discovered several stray dogs in and around many villages, that had been abandoned, had no food, and were riddled with of fleas and ticks. As an animal lover, I recalled the power of pets in my childhood and I knew I couldn't just stand there and watch these animals suffer. A few of my friends were fond of dogs as well, so we decided to rescue some. We fed, cleaned, protected them and grew very fond of them! We named one Ode after Odesa, and one Nikki after Nikolaev, a city in southern Ukraine. One was a vast grizzly dog. We managed to remove thirteen ticks from his fur!

Witnessing the fear in the dogs from the constant bombardment was devastating. The sadness in their eyes was terrible – we could see their loneliness as they had not had any human contact for so long. It was one of the most heartbreaking things I had ever seen.

To get the dogs clean, we boiled some water and filled up old baths to give them a good old scrub. And that's when the founder of a popular dog walking app got involved.

The app was set up by former Army Commander Sonny D. Sonny and I had served together in the Rifles for many years and we were on tour together, in different companies. Sonny saw the posts I had put on Facebook about the desperate plight of these dogs and supported me by using his social media to get more attention.

We started to make plans to evacuate the dogs and do something extra in Ukraine; not just humanitarian aid, not just the training, not just holding the line, but trying to put some happiness into these dogs' lives. And in turn, helping the dogs made us happy. This work gave us another reason to wake up in the morning. They gave us a lot of love and attention, but the sadness in their eyes was soul-destroying. In the end, we had to pass on the rescue and evacuation of the dogs to a Canadian guy who was not contracted or fighting, but helping with training. Later on, he managed to get several dogs out of the war zone.

As we looked after the dogs, it provided us with the kick in the ass to do something meaningful as quite often, there were times where we just laid in bed. As mentioned, you would hear the mortars' thump in the distance. You would count them as per the army training. You count the splashes – *boom, boom, boom* – and then louder – *boom, boom, boom*. And you thank God that none got too close.

Sometimes I would lie there thinking the next one will land on our house; at times, they almost did. We then just thanked our lucky stars that they didn't land on us. And once the *thump thump* disappeared, we would hear this almighty barrage behind us, which were our guys. That's the one that scares the shit out of all of us – making us jump because it was right behind us. But when we heard the whistling over the tops of our heads, we knew it was from our side, not the enemy's. That was an almighty relief. Of course, this could go on for hours.

It reached a point where I felt that I couldn't just sit around all day and wait for it to be over because it could end up being all day, and nothing would ever get done. Therefore, we all had our daily chores. We washed, cleaned our clothes and made something to eat – sometimes even a slap-up meal. The noise would descend around us as we cooked our sausage with pasta and tomato sauce. I would smoke a cigarette and then venture out to clean and feed the dogs. We always ensured our weapons were pre-primed and our batteries ready to go when needed. And, of course, we always ensured we had brushed our teeth!

We had our day-to-day routine going on, and artillery bombs were going off, left, right and centre, all around us. It reached the stage where we learnt to joke and laugh it off because what else can you do? As a soldier, you can do nothing other than find cover and hope nothing lands on you. It's one of the worst things about soldiering. You can sometimes spot an IED. You can deactivate and avoid minefields. You can react to enemy fire and know you can get out of a place and dodge a tank. But when the artillery comes down, it's just potluck. You hope and pray that it doesn't land on you. But when it does, and it has, it's pretty terrible. Even if you are not hit by flying shrapnel or killed by the base wave or heat wave, you become deaf. It knocks you for six, and the impact leaves you feeling disorientated.

I will never forget how quickly the situation could change so quickly in Ukraine. With all the commotion and madness that war brings, it is easy to lose track of time. One moment we were providing humanitarian aid and rescuing dogs, and in the next, we found ourselves plunged into the theatre of war and fighting for *Freedom at All Costs*.

Faithful friends!

Removing a tick from one of the
traumatised dogs.

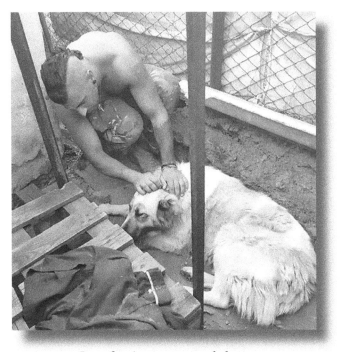

Comforting a rescued dog.

Scan the QR code to see a
heart-warming moment of me
with a scared dog.

A bit of normality in a war-torn environment.

August 2022

Love in Ukraine!

Do you believe in such a thing as fate? I do. Sometimes there are good things we can't imagine happening to us during tough times.

The problem with soldiers is when non-military guys join the services in voluntary roles, with no armed forces experience, they don't have that military discipline or a Band of Brothers attitude. It's more about what they can get out of the situation, so it becomes a struggle and they become a liability. Of course, after a while, some non-militaries prove themselves to be an asset and might even gel as a team, but it's only a few. Many of them hold you back and either become a problem, argumentative or exhibit selfish traits that threaten the unit's safety and don't help the cause.

I remember one time when I had time off before joining the Special Forces. There were a mix of men from different backgrounds with a less than positive attitude, resulting in useless arguments, which impeded the team's gelling, which is essential, as mentioned. When you have a group of misfits, it becomes problematic to lead a team mixed with professional and unprofessional soldiers. I want to stress that it is not that they didn't want to fight, but more about their argumentative ways and lack of discipline. The challenge intensified because many Ukrainians were civilians and had only been in the military briefly.

The untenable situation became too much for many men, and before long, I left with a small group of men. As a leader, I outlined what it takes to be successful and stay safe, so I made it clear to my soldiers that I'd give everybody another chance. I needed to set a deadline, so I gave them time to gel and put the childish bickering behind us. One of the aspects that I struggled with was that I found it rather embarrassing when you had the Ukrainians looking up to you as an expert and supporting their cause. The tiller pointed towards a breaking point, and I had to leave.

This decision was not easy because as I left them behind, some men became somewhat bitter towards me, and it caused many issues. As they stewed in their disappointment, one mentioned that he was unhappy about me leaving and vowed to bring me down. It fuelled bitterness and disappointment and caused much trouble with the unit I led. The resentment reached a boiling point when the unit commanders would not speak to me because of defamation of character and other related problems. This private assassination was a real issue because everything I had built was disintegrating.

I believed someone relatively new in the unit pulled my name through the mud and even persuaded some of the trusted friends I'd made along the way to turn against me.

After about four weeks of trying to communicate with the commanders in Mykolaiv, I realised they were unwilling to talk to me or my other colleague. Therefore, I decided to cancel the contract, and it was time to go our separate ways.

I decided to take a break in Odesa for some R&R to get away from the recent troublesome situation. It allowed me the time to reflect on what I had left behind in Lviv.

It was a summer's day, and I had some time off but was still in uniform. I was idly going around the shops browsing, enjoying the moment. I decided to go into this particular salon-type shop. As I walked in, I noticed a lovely girl behind the counter. She looked approachable, so I first hovered around, pretending to be interested in some products. I decided it was now or never to approach her. Summoning some courage, I walked towards the counter but saw she looked flustered, shocked and probably a little scared. I suppose I was a strange man in uniform, speaking English with a funny accent. I was on a mission, so I knew I should continue. I began talking to her about not very much because I wanted to put her at ease and make her realise I was one of the good guys.

I continued chatting, and after finishing my purchase, I asked for her phone number. Unbeknown to me, you do not ask Ukrainian women for their phone numbers!

Instead, if they like you, they will offer to give you their Instagram account. Oh, what a modern digital world we live in! If you are lucky, you soon realise their phone number will be in their Instagram account. Another reason it was awkward was that she spoke in broken English, interspersed with Ukrainian and Russian.

When I left and moved out to the front line, I couldn't find her on Instagram. Her name was spelt in Russian, and I was trying to spell it in English. So no Instagram chat ensued, and I discovered later that it had annoyed her as she thought I was ignoring her deliberately!

After my stint on the front line, I returned to Odesa and that particular shop, hoping she would be there again. Luckily for me, she was looking more beautiful than I had remembered. After grovelling and trying to apologise and explain in English, she gave me another chance.

From that moment on, we began to talk more and more on the phone, and soon, she became my go-to person, my confidant. I could speak to her about anything. There was no judgement. Not before long, we began to FaceTime, and I would call her during the lapses on the front line. She was my ray of sunshine and hope during those long, lonely and terrible days.

Meeting Helen was fate!

After spending some time with Helen, it was time to think about my next steps. I had left one group and was now searching for another Band of Brothers.

I remember being sent on a reconnaissance mission to gather information; this particular mission was executed by a small group actively involved in enemy lines. There were three of us and three Ukrainians, so only six. It is essential to go in small groups because you are pushing very close to the enemy. One of the requisites of these small groups is to get out of dangerous situations quickly because, more often than not, you don't have any backup.

The next decision involved pushing down to the target, as our mission was to establish the quality and quantity of their armour. After travelling a few kilometres, we jumped out of the vehicle into the treeline. It wasn't like the other times when we would run for cover and hide from possible sightings by the Russians; this time, it was far more dangerous. Great care was required because there were mines everywhere. But our trained eyes spotted them instantly. There were anti-tank and anti-personnel mines, so we had no alternative but to stick to a rigid treeline. Luckily for us, the path had been created by the Ukrainians, who had walked up and down it numerous times. We felt confident that it was pretty safe.

On missions like this, it was incredibly reassuring to be equipped with the correct kit - our anti-tank weapons, rifles and night-vision goggles. The goal was to meet up with an observation point (OP). On arrival, I sat with them, intending to gather first-hand information. We patrolled a thin treeline, and to our right, we could see where the grass had been burnt and destroyed by fires owing to several battles. There was a distinct stench of smoke hanging in the air.

As we walked along a concrete irrigation ditch, we had to dart forward every time we came to an opening because we were vulnerable. Our easily recognisable shapes were silhouetted to the Russians. The first thought was to try and remain hidden, as we didn't want the enemy to know we were using the irrigation ditch. We patrolled for about an hour or so, taking our planned breaks. At one point, we took a left and continued with our regular patrol down a treeline.

We set up camp and started our routine on arrival at the OP. But there was nowhere for us to lie because the guys already there had taken all of the 'dug-in' positions. Eventually, we set up an observation rotation for an hour at a time. While one of us did the observation, the others rested. The rotation lasted an hour for each guy on observation. It was a round robin between the six of us.

Unfortunately, torrential rain started as evening fell, causing us to be stuck on the muddy ground. After a while, we were all thoroughly drenched and decided it was time to get into some cover. We knew space was tight, but there was just enough room for two guys to enter the hole. I decided to stay outside, under my poncho, on guard.

At one point, I heard some commotion. I could see two faint outlines moving up along the treeline in the distance. I called a couple of the others and we recognised night sights (infra-red that glow in low light, designed to allow a soldier to find and align their sights in the dark), but more distinctly, scopes, which are telescopic sights.

Next, we identified two guys in ghillie suits (camouflage armour with netting that the snipers wear). The snipers had seen our positions and sought to determine our reasoning for being there. We knew we were in a perilous position, as their next move would be to establish a situation where they could ambush us.

This cat-and-mouse game seemed to go on for an eternity, and after an hour or two, I was ready to move. As I stood in the rain, poncho over me, I relayed the information to the guys. I looked down the gangway, which was dug in precisely as a trench, waiting to see if the snipers would pop up. Muscles stiffened, breath held, I wondered if they were super ballsy enough to come so close. I thought possibly not, but I wouldn't take the chance as the other guys rested.

Next, I saw some flashes through the night sights. There were a couple of glares and I could see two guys crawling on their hands and knees – bloody hell, they came so close! I was expecting an ambush there and then. The rest of my team now stood to attention, waiting for the surprise attack.

There was a collective exhale of breath, as I think we did enough to spook them because they must have seen our scopes. Even when you believe there is a stand-off, your heart is still pumping and you sweat like crazy. We had prepared ourselves for close combat in the pouring rain. However, just as quickly as the enemy came close, they withdrew. At close quarters, seeing our numbers, they must have realised that it wasn't a good idea to come any closer as it would have been six against two. They knew we had noticed them, which was another reason for them to withdraw tactfully. But we remained on high alert throughout the night.

As daylight dawned, we saw their tanks patrolling in the distance, from left to right, right to left. Then they pulled up close, maybe fifty metres to our treeline, taking some pot shots at the treeline – they were very close to where we were, but they didn't know our exact position. It was incredibly noisy – *BOOM! BOOM! BOOM!*

After a few minutes, we debated whether we should take the tank out, but as we pulled forward with our anti-tank weapons, the tank had withdrawn and it was too late. At least we had the information we wanted, the pattern of life established and what kind of abilities and weapons they had. It was time to take the information back to headquarters. We patrolled back with some valuable information which led up to our next mission.

Our next mission was approximately one week after our close encounter with the snipers and tanks. With some hasty planning completed, three of us headed out on our mission. Two foreign fighters and I took the same route through the irrigation ditch I'd taken the week before, now flooded with water, and we channelled to the same position as our last assignment. The difference was that there were no Ukrainians amongst us this time, as we knew they would never push any further forward than our current position. We would have to take a massive risk to gather more information.

We decided to push a kilometre past the opposition's front line and venture beyond enemy defences along a treeline plus another core concrete irrigation ditch. With a knowing glance, we thought it would be safer to ditch any heavy kit: body armour off, helmets off.

Now, we were ready with minimal kit: ammunition, water and a poncho. The waterproof poncho was crucial because it would block heat from any drone.

We pushed forward as the sun set, hoping its glare would blind the Russians' eyes, giving us added protection from being sighted. Assuming tactical considerations in full reconnaissance mode, we were uncertain what to expect, yet prepared. We could be their target and fired upon at any minute. At one stage, we passed a group of trees and had our weapons trained on them, half expecting an ambush, but nothing happened, thank God.

Eventually, we reached the end of the drainage system, and again we were grateful for our safety and managed to arrive at our next position undetected.

We spent another night under the stars rotating observations. We lingered under the ponchos and felt the considerable risk because we were close to the Russians and their tanks. If they pulled up with one of these beasts, we'd never be able to outrun it.

However, it was the risk we were willing to take in exchange for vital information. We stayed there all night. It crossed our minds to stop for a few nights, but we realised that the tank would drive past at some point.

A debate ensued on whether to remain and wait for the tank, hit it and then bug out quickly. As we waited, our eyes noticed a tank looming through the darkness, coming closer and closer to us. To our horror, it didn't turn off, but patrolled only 100 metres away from us.

We realised that there were some observation posts in the distance. We worked out a rough estimate of what armour they had in their possession and gathered enough information to form an idea about the pattern of life. It was time to make a move, or we risked losing the cover of darkness, and in the morning light, we'd probably be in the shit. The ensuing decision made, we opted for a tactical withdrawal.

About three-quarters of the way into the tactical withdrawal, we heard a low rumble, which grew louder and louder and louder. We realised that the tank was pulling up and chasing us down! It's not a good feeling when there are only three of you with just rifles – nothing more – and a tank in full pursuit! Fight or flight takes over, and now survival kicks in; out of nowhere, it was as if a super-human power fuelled our next move.

We were running as fast as we could across open ground. We made the tactical decision not to run straight into the treeline where our observation post was, but instead, took a right and doglegged around the treeline so that the enemy didn't know our exact positions.

As the tank neared, it saw the treeline and pulled off about forty metres away. And then it opened fire – *BOOM!* – straight overhead.

It was fucking scary. Imagine a tank shooting at you when you are that close to it! We dived into cover. I plunged into a pit covered with leaves and muck and fell through just as a second shot fired. Again, it went straight over our heads. We tried to get our anti-tank weapons out but hesitated. They knew where we were, so we had no alternative but to push forward unless we wanted to go on a suicide mission. It was too risky to expose ourselves; being gunned down was not how this would end.

We were so close, and it felt like a missed opportunity. However, we took comfort that we now knew their positions. We had sufficient information for immediate transfer to the high command. Satisfied we had three successful missions under our belts, we returned to camp.

I believe things happen for a reason, and just by luck, when I was in Odesa, I met up with a guy forming a new team heading northbound for Kyiv to sign contracts for a full-time job with the Special Forces. He asked if I was interested in joining them, and I explained that I was dealing with my team right now but maybe in the future.

However, familiar emotions stirred, and the yearning to belong to a Band of Brothers returned, and I thought it would be a shame to waste this great opportunity. So when they offered me a position and a chance to sign a formal contract, I jumped.

He introduced me to two other guys, and one in particular called Daniel Burke. They had similar experiences and training to me, so it was a good omen.

The next day, we decided to meet for a serious conversation. During talking about our history in the British Army, it turned out that Daniel had trained alongside me sixteen years ago! And when Russia annexed Crimea illegally in 2014, Daniel founded Dark Angels, a group of international volunteers who want to help Ukraine in their fight for freedom. The whole concept of the Band of Brothers rekindled our friendship! I knew it was a sign of great things to come.

We started building a new team with qualified, decent soldiers willing to work and fight for Ukraine. We attracted guys who mirrored our principles and reflected the reasons we were there doing what we do best, protect and defend. The meeting was a real uplifting moment for me after the negativity that I'd experienced the previous month.

So after meeting them as arranged, we travelled to Kyiv for a few days and signed the contracts. Our instructions were to wait down in Odesa until called forward, so we headed back there to await our next move.

Ewen Cameron from ReactAid shows
the utter devastation.

A much-needed convenience store that has
been ruined by the wrath of Russian aggression.

Built-up areas where
civilians live are no refuge
from the might of the
aggressor's attacks.

Even family-friendly
McDonald's cannot escape
the ravages of the Russian
bombs.

Scan the QR code to witness the
shocking horrors of war.

Shallow graves reveal the horror of war in the
midst of civilian areas. The lack of respect for
both the living and the dead is palpable.

Alison and one of the Third Wave volunteers
in an underground bunker.

A downed helicopter – the wreckage of war.

The uncovering of mines in the long grass
shows that danger is never far away.

The weaponry of war.

Ukraine Army logo.

President Volodymyr Zelensky showing true
leadership and strength, offering support to
some of the Ukrainian troops.

September 2022

We gathered some provisions when we arrived in Odesa and settled in an old village. It was relatively sparse; we had no running water: just a well, an outhouse toilet belonging to an old abandoned house, and a chained-up dog, which we released. Having a deep connection to dogs, we fed and cleaned the dishevelled and flee-ridden dog and welcomed him in as one of our pets!

The next goal was to set up the home comfortably and quickly and adapt to our new surroundings. But within hours, we could hear a persistent buzzing noise of trucks and other vehicles on the move, and experience and knowledge told us that something was brewing.

The following day, we were introduced to the rest of the team, who we were there to train with our hastily put together training programme while integrating them into the team as part of the particular reconnaissance unit. Everything went well, and we felt confident and ready. We had our drones, ammunition and weapons, so we practised and prepared over the next few weeks.

The cottage itself had three rooms: one double room, one single room that led from one room to another with no passageway, and a makeshift kitchen. Although unsafe, we were lucky to get the gas fire working. Switching on the fire ignited a flame from the back of the tube, which fed into the fire. It was touch and go, but at least we had gas.

We fetched water in a bucket from the well and would boil it or wash with it. There is a saying, "Necessity is the mother of invention". We devised a system of suspending a watering can from the garage by a piece of rope. We found a large rectangular plastic basin where we would stand and pull the cord to pour the water over us. This gadget was our makeshift shower; an accomplished job!

I slept on the floor next to the window and hooked up all my gear beside my feet, making it easily accessible. Daniel had the large room next to mine as he had all the tech equipment, and Jack shared the room with me on the double bed. I remember him moaning that the bed was uncomfortable, and he wished he'd taken the floor!

The house appeared stuck in a time warp. Imagine some old-school painting with a single-storey building, plastered outer cottage walls with fields outback. There was another similar cottage next door and a single gravel path in the middle of nowhere. These buildings are painted in the typical Ukrainian blue wash with some old little square windows barely letting in any light.

We made ourselves comfortable, and soon our faces became known at the local shops. All the military men and women would hang around a small coffee shop that made fantastic pizzas, but there wasn't much else in this tiny hamlet. Just the big buzz of trucks and whatever else caught our attention.

The training days broke the monotony, and I was happy to continue my training programme. The men were mainly older veterans, so we didn't have to train them from scratch. It made my training easier than if they had been civilians. The advantage was they understood the military language, even though they spoke no or little English.

I trained them on patrol skills, shooting skills and hand signals. We worked on formations, walking through streets, and reacting to enemy fire through woodland and open ground. These activities were all basic soldiering skills. The men responded well to and enjoyed the training, including our connections. We were with a professional group, and it felt good.

We held grenade range days on occasion, throwing grenades at the targets. We would zero our weapons in the sun. Zeroing a weapon is when you adjust a gun or rifle so a target is in sight. We competed on who could hit the mark with the best accuracy at certain distances. All of these activities ensured a genuine camaraderie began to shape the group. I couldn't stop smiling; my gut told me I was in the right place, fulfilling my mission and making a difference. Once again, I could use many of my military skills and expertise to their potential. It felt great.

During this time, we had a call to confirm the complete preparation for our mission. It reminded me of the scene in the TV series *Band of Brothers* where they were all lining up with their kits, ready to jump in the practice of leaving, in the moment's tension, waiting for the pickup to move out, only to be told there would be no jump tonight. It was the same for us at times; there was no moving out today.

Finally, we realised something was about to happen when we heard the endless rumbling of the overnight trucks, tanks and BMPs (infantry fighting vehicles), maybe half a kilometre from the main road. All we could hear throughout the night was the rumbling, rumbling, rumbling of a never-ending convoy. We spotted them from a distance. We could hear the bombardment of artillery, which started in the early morning hours. We looked at each other, knowing that the big push had begun.

It was the hour we had been waiting for, so it was with calm and military precision that we prepared ourselves, ready to go.

Next, we were instructed to attend our commander's location for a briefing. His nickname was Sarmat but his real name was Andriy Orlov, and he was one of the most-decorated Ukrainian army heroes. Once we arrived, we collected more ammunition, anti-tank weapons, other munitions and the required kit. The briefing informed us that we would hold back from the tanks, wait for the main infantry to push forward, and then follow up behind, dismount and drive through the forest. Our job was to gain information on enemy positions, including their weapon capabilities and other vital evidence, to give us an advantage.

We arrived at the extraction point, where a small BMP waited. We engaged in some pleasantries: smoked a cigarette, bumped fists and shouted, "Let's get going, boys!" At last, we were on our way to the big push, our energies cumulating in an exhilarating yet intensely nervous drive.

It started to rain and the BMP kicked up all the mud. These conditions were our signal to put on our shades and face coverings. The swirling black smoke rising from each side of the BMP raised adrenaline levels but simultaneously filled you with a nerve-wracking sensation. Now and then, we'd peer over the van and one or two of the other lads were bumping fists. Voices rang out, "Everything's gonna be okay!"

We finally reached the infantry but had to back off because we had caught up too quickly and hit a choke point. A choke point is where anything moving, be it traffic or men, has to move through a smaller area or path and the traffic gets backed up and spotlights it as a highly vulnerable area. A few days before, the infantry had set up a small floating bridge so we could get across the river. Unfortunately, it rained heavily and the bridge was underwater. Faced with a submerged bridge, we stopped in our tracks. We had to wait for the infantry to repair it and check it was safe to use before being allowed to cross. We also had to consider that we were sitting ducks, resulting in our BMP moving back.

The bridge was finally fixed and cleared to cross. The tanks were all pushing up along the treeline and set up, ready for the next phase. They had successfully pushed the Russians back, who were now drawing their artillery and tanks back, retreating from the villages we were trying to overtake. With our small BMP, we crossed the river.

As we took a left, we drove past all the infantry and the Home Guard, and we saw some pretty gruesome stuff – several casualties, headless bodies, amputees and severely damaged vehicles. Seeing the carnage, it was evident that we missed much of the battle, but that wasn't our mission.

Looking around, other personnel were giving us fist bumps in the air, and that deep-knowing connection between men in combat zones felt good, despite the atrocities. As we drove past other vehicles in the woods, guys would raise their arms in solidarity. It felt great; there was a tremendous sense that, collectively, we were fighting for freedom, and we were fighting for this land. There was a sense of indestructible unity. It filled us all with strength and pride.

After fifteen minutes of rumbling around in our BMP, smoke was still kicking up and the vehicle was covered in mud. Everyone was freezing, soaked through to the skin. We stopped at a safe point and jumped off, pulling our kit off carefully and quickly.

Instructions presented informed us that there were two drop-off points, Rendezvous (RV) One, RV Two and an Emergency RV. From here, we had plenty of walking to do. We assumed all-around defence while the BMP reversed and returned to its next mission as it was too loud for us to use where we were going – our position was deep reconnaissance.

We organised our kit, made sure of our formation and patrolled off tracks, keeping quiet whilst looking out for the enemy. We needed to ensure the coast and way were clear for the infantry. Allotted our designated points, we rendezvoused with an infantry parallel to us, giving us the confidence that we were on the right track. We set up on top of a bone line – the brow of a hill already dug in.

All at once, two massive rockets came out of nowhere and hit a barn about 100 metres in front of us. I remember that the barn housed a combine harvester which was completely destroyed in a huge fireball of an explosion. Daniel shouted at me, "Amin! Get out of here!" and he pulled me into a trench saying, "You need to move faster than that, Amin!" I was actually in awe of the strength of the fire power. It once again reminded me of a scene from an action movie!

You could see the trenches already dug on the hill, but the trees were scorched and broken. The scene in front of us was one of complete devastation and destruction. I sat forward, looking over the brow of the hill and down at the village to try and glean as much information as possible.

We sent up a drone. As soon as the drone went up, two tanks pulled up out of nowhere, maybe fifteen metres behind us to the left and right. A barrage of artillery started hitting our positions – *BOOM! BOOM! BOOM!* They aimed for our tanks but landed twenty metres, thirty metres, fifty metres and one hundred metres from our posts.

The attack went on for quite some time. Our tanks returned fire, which made me jump out of my skin because you could see the earth and the gravel vibrate and fly off the ground. No matter how often you have heard the boom of a tank's artillery, it is always a jumpy experience having such a large vehicle behind you and not knowing when it will go off.

After some time, I looked around and realised my guys had pulled back, and I was left out in the open, observing alone, trying to get some information. However, whenever I popped up, I'd get splashed with mud, grit and dirt, so I kept my head down as much as possible and waited for a lull in the battle.

In a let-up in the firing, I jumped up, called for the lads, picked up the kit I had left behind and pulled back to the underground bunker where I initially jumped in. Knowing six were sitting alongside me, I felt less alone. I was unsure how much more protected we were while remaining underground, but it felt safer.

Our infantry had pushed forward rapidly, forcing the Russians back faster than we expected. Before patrolling ahead, we returned halfway back to HQ, located under some trees, for a new mission brief.

October 2022

The following mission brief was to pinpoint where all our spearhead troops were and ensure they were in the correct positions before we could proceed with our initial observations. In short, our next mission was to find our forces.

Incredibly, the same thing happened again. We rumbled back and forth in the BMP, then dismounted, checking the maps to see exactly where the troops should be, patrolling with a heavy kit which was soaked through, ensuring that we stayed on track and didn't bump into Russian forces.

It was growing dark as we approached the second village. A long road was before us, and we patrolled along its hardstanding as there were trees for cover from sight on each side. Still, the battle raged around us with guns and tanks firing from afar; we could see where artillery had struck the concrete as it was all torn up and cracked.

Every stretch of that road was strewn with some downed vehicle, whether a Russian tank, a Ukrainian car, a supply van, or an ambulance. This stretch was a kilometre of scorched ground, with upside-down, mangled cars and other abandoned vehicles. We could tell that a severe battle had taken place here. With no choice, we pushed forward, dodging these artillery strikes.

The only thing you can do in this position is to keep walking forward, staying as low as you possibly can, but with the amount of kit we were carrying, it was hard going. After a while, we reached a point where we met one of the brigade commanders who told us that there was no minimal push forward from this point. It was as far as we could go with our exploitation – meaning how far we could 'exploit' the area to set up sentries. There usually is a limit on a map of how far you can push or where your mission leads you.

The boys pulled us into a treeline, which reminded me of a harbour area in the basic training I undertook while I had served in the Rifles. A harbour area is where a group of soldiers will go into a woodland area and set up a boundary in lines. A hasty harbour is fast and set up in a triangle, so everyone faces outwards. The woods were mainly fir trees, making them very dense. One of the guys, Shum (Oleh Shumov), remembered a small stone cove bridge which would shelter us from the elements. He went down to check it out and confirmed there were mines surrounding an overturned abandoned vehicle, so he led us carefully, and we walked down the safe route one by one.

We saw an overturned Cossack vehicle, and for one nervous moment during the patrol, one of the boys pointed at the ground and said something in Ukrainian. I was carrying four rucksacks and I was exhausted. I mistakenly thought he asked me to put my backpacks down, and as I went to swing them off my shoulder, everybody screamed. I stopped in my tracks and they pointed at a mine. I couldn't believe it! I could have killed us all! So I stated that communication was vital for our safety; simply pointing at something was not enough. They had to tell me exactly what they meant. "Okay," the boys said, "next time we will shout, 'There's a mine!'"

Ultimately, we all laughed, breaking the tension, putting it down to experience and a lucky escape.

We trudged under the bridge on highly uneven ground, covered in bricks, rocks and gravel. We spent twenty to twenty-five minutes building small walls on each side before making the coffee. It was pretty cosy! We slept shoulder to shoulder, and I was close to 'the Professor' who was on my left, and we managed to get quite comfortable with sentries rotating around. It would be an early start in the morning, so "Good night, boys!"

As we were about to get our heads down, the bombardment from the Russians started again. Because of the bridge's echo, it sounded ten times closer. I swore at some point that these rounds were going through and under the bridge as the noise was deafening – no ear defenders here! They were aiming in our direction; somehow, most of the boys got some shut-eye.

The next morning, we were up bright and early, ready for the day's work to determine where our exploitation was. We intended to return to our original task of deep reconnaissance and assault.

Subsequently, we gathered our kit together, and at that point, Shum came running back from an area further down; he'd found several weapons, including six Javelins. We were very excited at these little trophies for ourselves, but unfortunately, we couldn't carry them all, so we only took a couple on board. I retrieved a tank destroyer and an anti-tank weapon, and the rest we buried carefully, checking for mines, of course...

We organised our kit and patrolled off as and when it was time to go. Zero six hundred hours, and off we went in a single formation.

We were patrolling again, up through the woods, this time on the open ground, leaving us pretty exposed, and I was not too keen on the area in which we found ourselves. It was open fields, perfect for tanks, with only small treelines. The distance was a mere fifty metres across and maybe a couple of hundred metres in length where another group of soldiers had dug in. They were like sardines, with little space to move around. But it was easier to target the enemy, so they had to win the firefight to push the Russians back. I did not feel happy for the boys we were passing, but we had to reach the limit of exploitation because we needed to communicate our findings with the commander.

As we were patrolling through the fields, we entered into the treelines. We were dubious and uncertain and felt we needed to drop some kit. We dropped off some gear with two of our men at specific points. We pushed forward again, and when we had almost reached our exploitation limits, we dropped off most of the rest of our kit. We heard that there was an eighty-metre space of open ground to get to our limit of exploitation. It was all becoming pretty uncomfortable.

Our men said they had seen two tanks, possibly a BMP and the infantry, about 100 to 200 metres away. It had never been my intention, nor was I planning on, being part of the front line spearhead troops, and it was mainly for reconnaissance that I signed up for, but unfortunately, it turned out this way. It was the last thing we needed to do before pulling back out and continuing our initial mission of finding the Russians, but at least we had found the front line and all our troops. Weighing everything up, I said, "Okay, let's go ahead."

Our armour then targeted the tanks. The Russian tanks pulled back, as well as their troops. We hadn't seen anything of the drone for a while, so on the count of three, six of us darted across the eighty metres of open ground under fire. We had covering fire from our troops – *tata tata tata tap*, *tata tata tata tap*, *tata tata tata tap* – and we managed to get across where we connected with the second reconnaissance group and the spearhead of that assault, which was a relief. All we needed to do now was confirm the enemy's positions and bug out; mission accomplished.

We sat down and realised that the grid shell had been incorrectly dug and remained unfinished. Consequently, one of the lads, Matt, said, "Stay here and look after the troops." I placed our boys in all-around defence and waited off to the left.

Matt pushed forward and set up the drone; next thing, all hell broke loose. I have never experienced anything like it in my entire life, not even in Afghanistan. The ferocity of firepower was mind-blowing.

Rounds rained down on us from artillery in every direction, then something exploded on a tree close to where we were. Sparks were flying everywhere; splinters of wood, branches and churned-up earth were all around us.

A loud and almighty bang made me jump out of my trench. I saw Shum fly forward, although seemingly protected by the tree in front of the one hit by firepower. My great pal, 'the Professor', dragged Shum in, and I helped him into a tiny trench. The Professor was beside him, hugging him. I said, "Shum! Have you been hit? Have you been hit?" The next thing we knew, more artillery rounds started hailing down on us.

Shoot, shoot, boom, boom, boom, boom! It was a heavy rate of fire. I had nowhere to take Shum, but I could see his arm was sodden with blood. I took out my medical pack, and as I was trying to cut his sleeve, I realised that the scissors I had were blunt! I managed to cut to the top of his shoulder. I checked him and asked him if he was able to breathe. He was, but he had been hit three times in the arm. It was a severe wound, blood gushing everywhere. It wasn't full-on catastrophic, but he lost a lot of blood.

First, I put pressure on the wounds and then stuffed them with Celox. Celox is a unique advanced bandage that stops lethal bleeding and seals wounds quickly. Even after the Celox, it still kept bleeding, so I applied a tourniquet. The tourniquet slowed the bleeding, but the blood was still coming, and I did not want to put another tourniquet on him.

As I dressed the wounds, rounds were shooting all around us. It was wild. I needed to get him wrapped up as fast as possible. While wrapping it, I noticed three direct hits in his arm, three holes. Then I detected another bleed on his wrist, so I wrapped the arm as best as possible. I was struggling to get the bandage hooked around his wrist. I said, "Sorry, Shum, you need to tuck that in and hold it tight. The bleeding should slow down; now, get into that trench!"

He tumbled into the trench. The Professor and I were stuck in a cot-sized buried dunk shell trench before us. A shell landed next to us as we ran forward, sending us flying. Luckily, we weren't hit. But we were heavily knocked off our feet. We dived back into the trench, picked up our weapons and scanned the ground. We couldn't see the enemy then, but we could see some small muzzle flash. I let off a couple of rounds in the direction of the enemy.

Suddenly, I had to get my head down because of incoming rounds and artillery; it was relentless. One after another, after another; the ground shifted, the trees exploded, and the only thing we could do was duck when they got too close. Every time a round went over our heads, the Professor would duck, and I would weave. We were helmet to helmet, as low as possible on our knees. We were not covered, and it had been raining for five days, so it was slippery, muddy and dangerous. Every time a round hit, it would be closer and closer to our spot.

This relentless badgering went on for about fifteen minutes.

When I thought there was a lull, I'd look up to see if there was anything I could do or anywhere I could go in an attempt to pull the guys back. No such luck, so unfortunately, the Professor would grab my hand and pull me back into a tiny little shell trench.

As darkness descended, it began to rain, and the shelling worsened. There was no let-up! I shouted to Professor, "Where are they getting all this ammunition?" This extreme situation was the front line of all front lines! And there was nothing I could do because there was open ground to the left, hollow ground to the right and open ground to the front. I realised the seriousness of my situation – I was cornered, and I thought it would only be a matter of time before I was hit...

Suddenly, another round hit, maybe four, five metres to my right. The whole ground shook and sucked the air out of our lungs.

I thought, *Well, that's not so bad,* because the next round would usually never land so close to the first one. But then an almighty thud and a blinding flash exploded before my eyes. It felt like someone had dragged me underground.

Someone had given us a direct hit.

The description I can offer you of how I felt will never do it justice.

I saw a red flash and felt sucked underground to the depths of hell. My whole body felt crumpled, like a tin can that someone had stood on. All the air was sucked out of my body; I felt totally compressed. And as I looked up, I still hadn't realised yet that we'd been hit. But I could see my brother, the Professor, flailing about as if he was floating in water. Both of his arms were out in front, and I must have been doing the same.

I looked down and realised I was barely breathing as everything returned to consciousness. *What is this new reality?* We'd both come down to earth. *Crash!* The Professor was on my back. I took a massive gasp of air. I could not believe it. I'd been hit and shouted in my head, *I've been hit! I've been hit!* Then I gasped, "Professor! Professor!" as I shook him.

Then I realised he was gone…

Discovering one of your unit is catastrophically wounded and another is dead fills you with guilt, and you ask yourself, *Why not me? I shouldn't be alive.* But I knew I had to get out of this trench or I would die here. I needed to get out, but nothing moved as I tried to push myself up. The Professor was lying on top of me, covered in rubble, and my weapon staked deep into the trench. I thought, *I'm dying here, and this is where I die.*

I didn't feel pain yet, but I was 100% sure I was going to die. Strangely, I was at peace with it. I hadn't realised why I hadn't died immediately. I was waiting for that energy to drain away, and it just didn't drain away. I wondered why I was not dead yet. It didn't make any sense to my befuddled brain. *Am I going to have a painful death? What is going to happen to me?* And then I came to, and I felt better. Maybe I wouldn't die after all.

I tried again to get out of the trench, but it was too slippery with the rain, and the mud wedged me in, and then it struck me – I was having difficulty breathing.

I called out to Shum, not expecting him to be alive, and I listened for a distant voice. "Shum, are you alive? Are you alive?"

He shouted, "Yes!"

"I've been hit, and Professor is on top of me, and I am stuck! Can you help me?"

He jumped out of the trench, and almost immediately, the rounds started coming down again; machine gun fire and artillery. *Boom… Boom… Boom…*

He ran towards the Professor, grabbed him by the straps from behind, pulled him back and ran back into his trench as quickly as possible.

My injured hero, Shum, still under fire, with a badly injured arm, risked his life by jumping out of the trench to rescue me, and for that, I will be forever grateful – I owe my life to Shum.

Mustering all of my remaining strength, I tried to push up from either side of the trench with my arms, and as I did, an almighty pain surged through me. I felt an almighty fucking agony through my lungs and arm. I looked down, and my hand was hanging off. I had my belt kit around me, my body armour, everything on me.

As I tried to use it, I realised my arm was broken and useless. I had not realised that my whole arm was shredded. I tried to push up with my right leg, and as I looked down, I saw a substantial piece of metal curling from left to right, a metal shaving about four inches by six inches, through one end of the inside of the leg coiling round and coming out the other side of my leg. "This is not going to work," I said to myself.

Then at that moment, I heard my commander in the background. By now, it was growing darker and the rain lashed down. He shouted, "You've got to get yourself out of that trench!" I wondered what the point of my past gym work was if I could not get myself out of the trench!

So with every last inch of breath and power I had in my left leg and left arm, I grabbed onto the outside of the trench. I first unclipped my belt buckle, gripped onto the mud, and pulled. I screamed ... rolled onto all fours, and crawled out of the trench. The darkness was the thought that flooded my mind, and the next thing, *papapapappapapppaaa*, repeating shots echoed to my left.

Bang! Another almighty pain, and sure enough, I'd been shot in the left arm or had a ricochet bullet. This new wound made life more difficult because I could only use my shoulder and left foot to push myself and try to find some cover. I said to myself, "Reef, you need to get to that tree." But I just couldn't do it. I was sliding backwards in the slippery mud.

Suddenly I was grabbed by my straps and dragged onto my back, and my commander pulled me away into some cover as the rounds thrashed down in the pouring rain.

I shouted, "You need to get me off these rocks! I'm lying on rocks here and I'm in agony!"

The commander replied, "They're not rocks; that's metal in your back! It's your body armour that is still on you. The blast went down at your feet and punched about nine feet underground. The wet and clay-like ground took the blast, designed to uproot soldiers from under the ground. But the explosion went upwards instead of outwards and went inside your armour. I need to put some tourniquets on you, but I've got no pain relief."

He applied the tourniquets to my right leg and right arm. I can only describe the pain as unimaginable, like being hung, drawn and quartered from the olden days. I could almost cope with the pain of the injuries. But once those tourniquets went on, that's when the screaming started. That's when the pain started, and I knew, as a medic, that you have to pull tight no matter how loud and hard the screams are.

I looked down at myself in the pouring rain and it felt very surreal – like I was in some Hollywood movie.

Matt appeared in his trench coat with his walkie-talkie. I was trying to catch my breath; my breath was becoming shorter and shorter by the minute. I knew this was the critical moment, the Golden Hour as it is known; the pain surged through my legs, lungs, hands and arms; everywhere. Matt turned around and said, "Don't worry; one way or another, I'll get you out of here."

Then I heard him speaking in Ukrainian on the radio to one of the Cossack vehicles we had been exploring earlier. After about fifteen minutes, I heard a loud, deafening rumbling in the background. I don't understand how I was still conscious. One of the Cossack vehicles appeared with six guys in ponchos, who slid me onto another poncho and threw me into the vehicle's back end with Shum. I'm not sure if the Professor came with us. It was as if they were throwing a sack of potatoes, but it didn't matter at that critical moment. We all needed to get out of the area as quickly as possible. They turned the vehicle and drove like hell for leather across open ground.

While on the floor and under fire, I remember the Cossack rumbling and ammunition rounds ricocheting off the vehicle's side. The car bounced about as it rolled across the uneven terrain. It was cold and dark, and I was in absolute agony.

I told the guys I was struggling to breathe. They sat me up and pulled off my body armour. They used some compression needles in my ribcage to try and release the gas. It was painful, but I didn't care. I just wanted to breathe!

We had been driving for about twenty minutes when the vehicle stopped, and I thought, *Thank God, we're at the hospital.* To my absolute horror, we had only driven to a field ambulance. They bundled me into the ambulance, and the medics asked, "How do you feel? What's wrong?"

I gasped, "I can't breathe." They realised that my lungs had been filling up with gas and blood. It was only a matter of time before my lungs would pop and I would drown, so they tried more compression needles, but it was too late for that.

They had to insert two large spiked tubes into each lung. I remember having one arm up and being stabbed deeply in the lower left side with a line that would drain the blood from my lungs, and then the same to the upper side. And then, all of a sudden, the blood drained, and I could slowly feel my breath returning to almost normal breathing. The procedure was the most considerable relief for me as being able to breathe was the most vital thing!

It took another fifteen to twenty minutes before the ambulance stopped and I was chucked onto a trolley and rolled into the field hospital.

What stuck most in my mind when I arrived was hearing one of the surgeons, doctors or nurses saying in English, "He's not going to make it!" God knows why they would speak in English; perhaps they didn't realise I was English. Or maybe they said it in English so the Ukrainians wouldn't understand it. But unfortunately, I heard it, and I understood it. It wasn't very comforting.

I had been awake for maybe an hour and twenty minutes after being hit and I was still alive, completely conscious, and without pain relief.

I remember getting onto the operating table. It was so surreal. The medics were talking over me and shining a bright light across the top of the table. A nurse said, "I'm going to put some air on you." Then they cut all my clothes off. Their action seemed frantic but theoretically methodical as they did this daily. I would call it organised chaos.

They placed a gas mask over my face, and for the second time that night, I felt that was the last thing I would ever see. I thought, *I'll never wake up. I'm okay with the situation and have surrendered to my fate.* I have heard that when you think your number is up, things are put onto perspective.

My injuries were extensive. My right hand was destroyed, my arm was shredded and my shoulder was gravely damaged. The top of my left arm was broken, and I had shrapnel in my right leg. I had nerve damage to the knee, shrapnel in my stomach, and exposure to the abdomen. Large bits of shrapnel were found in my body, spine and collarbone. I had roughly twenty pieces of shrapnel removed. Both of my lungs collapsed and filled with blood. "Oh God – am I going to live?"

Somehow, I managed to escape death. I still believe that there is a bigger purpose for me. My life has yet another purpose to fulfil. I knew I had to survive to continue the fight for *Freedom at All Costs.*

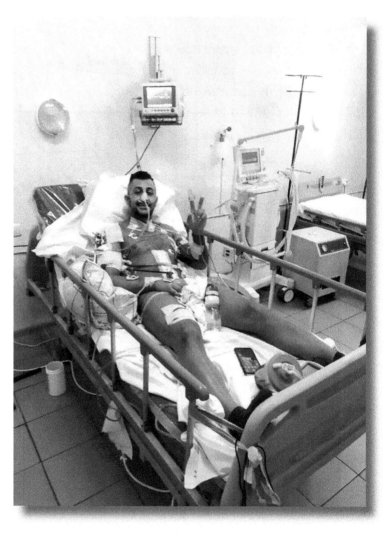

In hospital in Odesa. My injuries were horrific.

On the mend – despite my terrible injuries,
I am still defiant.

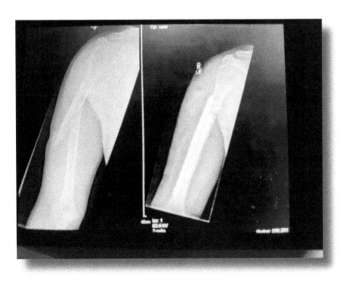

The extent of my arm injuries –
before and after…

November 2022

I do not remember much of November.

I was in constant pain and had many different operations to try and repair my hand and right arm. I was drugged up to the eyeballs on morphine and other medication.

I suffered two punctured lungs and significant injuries to every single limb in the battle. The British Army trained me for such eventualities, and I knew that as a troop, you work together. I was left wondering what had happened to my brothers in arms. I later learnt that Shum fully recovered from his arm injury.

Three pieces of the shrapnel removed from my body sit in a glass jar beside my bed. I feel blessed and thankful that I am still alive. Even in my desperate state, I was lucky because I was found and rushed from the front line to the hospital. My injuries were so extensive that the medics feared I would lose my right hand and arm, and would not make it.

At first, it seemed that fate dealt a cruel blow to me. When I left the UK to come to Ukraine, it was not because I wanted to fight on the front lines, it was more about the humanitarian side of war and teaching the civilian troops how to keep safe and protect themselves and their villages. At first, I was happy to carry out humanitarian work. I swiftly moved on to training civilian troops before I deployed to fight, and soon afterwards, my brigade came under intense fire during deep reconnaissance. Yet the irony is that I was a victim of hailing bullets and artillery and being blown off my feet in a chilling battle with the aggressor – Russian troops.

Many people call me a war hero and refer to me as 'Rambo', especially the media, which seems surreal because we all live to survive and thrive when we are free. That was my fight and the real reason I left the comfort of the UK to risk everything to support and help the Ukrainians fight for their right to freedom.

Sometimes you must sit up and face what life chucks at you, good and bad. I was awarded a medal for bravery, but I've no regrets about coming to Ukraine. I couldn't sit by, stick a flag on Facebook and a fiver in a fundraiser. What's that going to do? If I sat at home twiddling my thumbs, despite having skills that could help, what kind of human being am I?

My dad was a great role model because I remember, as a young boy and man, witnessing his determination to do what others had told him he couldn't. It was the same for me when doctors warned me that I may not walk again, and naturally, I defied them and walked.

I thank God my life has taught me to be tough during adversity and challenges. The inner strength is my saving grace, preparing me for the long recovery days ahead. I do not doubt that others see my toughness like Sylvester Stallone's 'Rambo', hence my nickname.

I survived a hail of Russian bombs and bullets, and despite some sadness at leaving Ukraine, and my Band of Brothers, I looked forward to returning home to be rebuilt.

December 2022

December in Ukraine continued with uncertainty as operation 'Take Me Home' was underway. It was not *if* I was going home, but *when*. Ukraine is full of bureaucracy, and every little piece of paper and detail needs a blue stamp.

Coming Home

Odesa to Rzeszów to Germany to Bristol

The BBC's Emma Vardy helped me get home and filmed a piece on me for the BBC Our World programme, *Brits in Battle: Ukraine*.

The operations in hospital in Odesa never ceased; sometimes, it would be two or three a day. I felt like a junkie, constantly drugged up with anaesthesia and painkillers.

After many complications, Ewen Cameron and Craig Borthwick from ReactAid reached me at the hospital in Odesa.

Ukraine Air Rescue was going to fly us all out, but we had to get across the border to Rzeszów, Poland, which was all somewhat unbelievable. Rzeszów Airport is a transshipment hub for Ukraine's civil, NGO and government supporters to resupply Ukraine with medical aid, weapons and supplies. Weapons and medical supplies are flown to the airport and driven across the Polish-Ukrainian border in trucks.

In Rzeszów, we met Emma Vardy and her camera crew, and they found us somewhere to rest whilst we waited for the plane.

Once the aircraft arrived, the combat medic equipment from the UK was unloaded and sent to the front line to help as many people as possible. My partner Helen and her son took a commercial flight whilst myself, Ewen, the medics and Emma boarded the Ukrainian Air Rescue jet. We had a quick refuelling stop in Germany, then later landed at Bristol Airport in the UK.

As my rescue was underway, we learned that the air team had managed to evacuate eighteen children with cancer out of Ukraine.

At the time of writing this chapter, it has been several months since my war injury. I was airlifted to the UK and admitted to Bristol's Southmead Hospital for reconstruction surgery on the NHS.

Consequently, the surgeons intended to repair and rebuild me. They talked about rebuilding one of my thumbs out of one of my toes and removing an artery from a leg to replace one under my forearm. In addition, they wanted to rebuild my shoulder and give me more mobility in my right leg. It would be best to find the funny side in life; otherwise, you could go mad. If they had already called me Rambo and the doctors intended to rebuild me, why not go from Rambo to Robocop?!

When you have inner strength and toughness, you can understand that I am determined to return to Ukraine to help the war effort. I want to be up and running and back on the ground to help however I can. Some people might call me 'mad' or even irresponsible, but despite what's happened, I'd do it all again in a heartbeat.

Ewen and Craig of ReactAid rescuing me
from the hospital in Odesa.

On the train from Odesa.

The BBC's Emma Vardy assisted in my rescue.

Ewen and Craig from ReactAid with Emma Vardy.

A break in the long journey!

With Emma, Craig and Ewen by the rescue plane.

The last leg of a long, hazardous journey.

A very tired trio on their way back to the UK.

Getting off the plane at Bristol Airport.

Home to Bristol at last! Here I am with
air co-ordinator Fiona Knight, Craig, Ewen
and the two pilots, Yannick and Max.

Article about my rescue in *The Daily Record*.

With my dad Laith at the hospital in Bristol.

ReactAid's Mission

This chapter recounts the story of Shareef's rescue by Ewen Cameron, Founder of ReactAid, and Craig Borthwick, Medic Trainer and former firearms specialist. It is worthy of a book for the danger and risk they both took to ensure Shareef arrived back safely in the UK.

I set up ReactAid in March 2022 in response to the Russian invasion, initially transporting goods and medical supplies to Ukraine. Since then, our aid effort has grown into a humanitarian operation which sees me and my team deliver support to communities across Ukraine, including organising Shareef's flight home with Ukraine Air Rescue.

We set about bringing vital supplies into Ukraine hospitals and to medics on the ground. We then moved into evacuations. It was an honour to be able to help Shareef. We've evacuated hundreds of people to safer lands so far and supported thousands in the country with medical and humanitarian aid. But we can only do so with the public's help via donations.

In addition, I trained to become a certified medic – handling pre-hospital care – and have branched out into air evacuations to the EU and UK after forming links with pilots in Poland.

I see my efforts in Ukraine as helping those living during the war, but also the future of my own and other people's children in a democratic and free society.

ReactAid is a humanitarian organisation that helps and supports brave humans who stay to help and volunteer. ReactAid aims to make pre-packed backpacks and deliver them through supply chains and logistics to troubled areas worldwide. The packs contain items the recipients requested, and many are currently in Ukraine.

Over time, ReactAid has evolved into working with a team of medical professionals who supply hospitals and doctors still in the country with much-needed medical supplies. We continue delivering food, water and other essential items to those with nothing.

Life has a fascinating way of bringing people together. Sometimes it appears fleeting, but the 'real' reason often becomes apparent.

Rob Paxman is the man in the middle who knew both me and Shareef. Rob ran PSS (Paradigm Security Solutions), which is how he got to know Shareef, who had worked with him before going to Ukraine. Rob told me all about Shareef's story and the severe injuries he received while in action on the front line in Ukraine.

When Rob brought Shareef's plight to my attention, we became involved in his evacuation. His injuries were far beyond what they could cope with in Ukraine, as they had limited antibiotics, supplies, expertise and equipment. Shareef's injuries and situation were exactly the support we love to provide and spur us on to evacuate casualties.

I met Craig Borthwick on social media, where we spoke and became very friendly. Craig did his own thing then, and ReactAid focused on their activity. Slowly, during our conversations, the idea of medical evacuations came about. When Shareef contacted ReactAid, I wanted Craig to help as I knew it would be a problematic evacuation.

Without hesitation, Craig Borthwick and I created a plan. With our extensive experience and expertise in both training the police and mountain rescue in firearms and medical support in trauma, hostile and austere environments, ReactAid could guarantee outstanding service and success rates for the rescue work we did. Craig had been in Ukraine right from the start of the war, acting as a medic before he became involved in teaching the military. He was involved in tactical medical training in Lviv at the military bases. He taught tactical medicine to the regular military, Territorial Army, Civil Defence Forces and Special Defence Forces, alongside teaching ex-US Special Forces. He was responsible for preparing the V40 medical battalion.

Tactical medicine is associated with an environment with risk and therefore needs to be conducted in a particular manner. At the start of the war, Ukrainian forces were repelling the Russians and pushing them out of Kyiv,

Bucha and other towns and cities where fighting was happening in built-up areas. Many houses were severely damaged, so the Ukrainians had to go from house to house to check for injured people and Russian troops.

Those involved had to learn what it takes to be a medic. It is important to remember that these people, particularly the volunteer medical battalion, were made up of doctors, dentists, nurses, vets and ambulance technicians. Whilst these people had medical experience, they had no medical experience of this specific trauma or the different tactics involved in moving through buildings and using a firearm. Using our knowledge and expertise, we taught them about tactical medicine. We taught them how to go through and clear buildings safely. We showed them how to set up areas within facilities to deal with casualties, as there were many casualties at that time.

It was problematic as we had to think clearly about the medical assistance required for Shareef's return trip to the UK. Another challenge was that we knew we had to travel far into Ukraine, which meant we would 'get our feet wet'. We couldn't have gone any further; we could see Russian-occupied territory from the edge of Odesa! Once Craig understood the mission, I asked him if he wanted to be involved, and he said, "Yes."

We created an excellent plan. However, the best laid plans… like everything else in this fast-moving war, things change rapidly and one has to adapt quickly. The initial plan was to meet in Kraków, pick up an ambulance, and drive to Odesa. At best, it would take fourteen hours, but bear in mind that Ukraine was then in the depth of winter

– around 17th December – there was a lot of snow, and the roads were untreated. The further east and south we went, the streets were damaged because of all the shelling and bombing. We weren't particularly looking forward to the long hazardous drive down to Odesa because we knew there had to be a quick turnaround. With all of this in mind, we also had to remember that Odesa was still heavily bombed, which could impact the quick turnaround.

Another primary concern was that the return journey of fourteen hours for Shareef in the back of an ambulance was not ideal for a man with the severity of his injuries.

Our first step was to get to Ukraine so we flew to Kraków in Poland. After careful planning, including being in touch with the Foreign Office and Ukraine Air Aid and ensuring all the necessary paperwork was in place, Craig was the first to arrive in Kraków. I then reached Kraków at about 10 p.m. the following night.

We had no time to waste, so we picked up the ambulance covered in two feet of snow! As you can imagine, parked in the freezing snow, we couldn't get it to start, but we were lucky enough after a while to get someone who could thankfully give us a jump-start. We drove off, heading towards Lviv down the motorway, where we planned to stay overnight in Medyka on the Polish-Ukraine Border because we knew we wouldn't arrive until four o'clock in the morning.

There are many challenges during rescue missions, and Shareef's was full of them. The challenges were even more arduous as we plunged into minus seven and eight degrees. At those sub-zero temperatures, everything was freezing; keeping the windows clear was particularly difficult, especially as we had to deal with all the mud from the roads. We were only twenty-five kilometres into the journey when we stopped at what we thought was a petrol station; it wasn't. We got some water that we thought would help, but it didn't, as it froze up again; but we did our best in the circumstances.

We needed fuel, so we drove another few kilometres. It was forty-four kilometres into the journey; I will never forget that. We turned off the engine and went to the petrol station. We took comfort in the fact that the ambulance had been running so it would have had a chance to charge the battery. We filled up with fuel, grabbed a coffee and returned to the ambulance, which, surprise, surprise, refused to start. It had died on us!

Luckily, we bumped into a few British fighters going down to volunteer with the Legion. They had jump leads which we tried, but unfortunately, they didn't work. We stopped a member of the public with a bigger car and hoped their car would start the ambulance, but to no avail. By this time, we were now in the early hours of Sunday morning. We knew where we were, but it was literally the middle of nowhere!

We were still in Poland, well below freezing, in the middle of the night, and we had some way to go, so the situation was not ideal, nor did it reflect our plans. The lesson from these experiences is: you learn to have contingency plans.

Many people would have given up, but we are both hardcore and Scottish; giving up is not an option! There was too much at stake. We decided to grab some more coffee and figure out our next step. A convoy of four SUVs turned up quickly with Ukrainian flags in the windows. Our first thought was, "Let's hope they speak English!"

It turned out that they were Ukrainians who lived in the UK and were delivering these vehicles to the 93rd Brigade. Ukrainian women would come across the border to collect these vehicles as the drivers were prohibited from crossing the Polish border into Ukraine.

These guys did some work on the ambulance, and we eventually had to arrange for a recovery truck to come out and pick it up, but it would not take us to Medyka. Ultimately, we abandoned the ambulance and tried to determine our next move.

Thanks to the supporters of the 93rd Brigade, we reached Ukraine. They drove us to the border between Poland and Ukraine, where we finally arrived at 6 a.m. Now we could get back on track with our rescue. They took us to a safe house that Ukrainians had set up for people to use, which we were very thankful for. They helped us and got us a room for the night, well, for a few hours!

We were fortunate enough to have the opportunity to consider and adjust our plans accordingly. After all, we were on a time restriction because we had to meet the plane provided by Ukraine Air Rescue that would fly us back to the UK. The crew were currently in Cologne,

215

awaiting our instructions. Craig got his head down for about an hour while I tried to source an ambulance to get us across the border into Ukraine.

Things weren't going so well, plus carrying 100 kg of kit and baggage across the border from Poland into Ukraine was no mean feat. Everything we were experiencing created tension from many angles. Getting into Ukraine was terrible enough, but getting back out is another story yet to be revealed.

We managed to get one of Craig's contacts to pick us up from the border to travel to Lviv. Everywhere we went, tremendous gratitude and generosity from the Ukrainian people followed. Yet another hotel, paid for by our contact, where we could freshen up and have food. Meanwhile, more decision-making was necessary as we explored what options would enable us to reach Odesa. I spent a lot of the time continuing to source an ambulance to get us all back across the border into Poland once we had picked up Shareef.

A source of Craig's from the refugee place managed to get us a lift to the border, which we crossed carrying all our kits. On the other side, Craig had sourced yet another ride to take us to Lviv. This time, it was a security organisation who were operating in Ukraine. They dropped off American senators at one border, and then they came to pick us up from the Medyka border, drove us down to Lviv, and kindly arranged a hotel for the night.

On the drive down, the guys told us an overnight train to Odesa existed. We checked online but were unable to find any trains that night. By now, exhaustion had set in as we'd had no sleep or a decent meal for almost two days. But then, as if by magic, we discovered a train that night leaving from Odesa, so we scrapped getting our heads down in the hotel and decided to head straight to the station to get the train.

You would think that getting a taxi to the station would be straightforward, but no, it gave us yet another headache. The train station was about twenty-five minutes away, and our taxi didn't turn up when we thought it would. When we organised the cab, we had thirty minutes spare, but we found ourselves in another stressful situation with the taxi failing to appear. Finally, it arrived with thirty minutes to go before the train left.

It was not as straightforward as jumping into a taxi because we had so much kit. While picking up the equipment and getting organised, a drunken woman appeared out of nowhere and claimed the cab was for her! Of course, we had the most bizarre conversation over this taxi, but we soon realised she would not budge! However, if we were to miss this particular train, it would delay us by another day. Not a good situation as we were on a time restriction due to the plane waiting for us, and we had yet to travel fourteen hours to and from Odesa as well as the time it would take to pick up Shareef...

We managed to get another taxi with twenty-three minutes to go until the train was leaving. The taxi driver was amiable and thanked us for everything we did for his country. The drive was horrendous as he manoeuvred many obstacles, but he was determined to get us to the train on time.

At last, the driver drove us right up to the train station. We unloaded the car, grabbed our tickets and looked for an ATM, as we had no money and needed to pay for the taxi. The driver would hear nothing of it and gifted us the white-knuckle ride for free.

We lugged our kit as best we could (all 100 kg) and ran through the station while trying to find the train to Odesa. At last, we boarded the carriage, only to be faced with a stern-looking female ticket conductor who refused to let us stay on the train. She asked to see our tickets, which were on my phone. Gasping for breath, I showed her our tickets. Meanwhile, I thought, *I feel like I'm going to have a heart attack at this rate, and now we are faced with yet another difficult situation.* When were we going to get a break?

The conductor was having none of it… she started screaming at us in Ukrainian, which we could not understand. Craig told her, "It doesn't matter how loud you scream at us; we still don't know what you are saying!"

Luckily there was a young girl next to us who was Ukrainian and spoke perfect English and was on her way to Odesa to see her boyfriend. It was a bit scary as this battleaxe of a woman had brought a male guard along, so we were expecting to be thrown off the train.

Thankfully, after a few exchanges, the situation seemed to calm down. Some normality was welcome to lighten the mood. We settled down and were soon on our way to Odesa.

There is much risk in travelling by train in Ukraine. Train stations make easy targets for the Russians, and some of the cities we passed through were at risk of being bombed, and one of the cities was attacked as we travelled through it. Having British passports gave us a relatively safe passage, especially when I could show them my medical badge.

We finally arrived in Odesa, which had suffered a bombing about an hour before. The whole city was in darkness with no power or water. We met a group of Ukrainian Special Forces at the train station who were travelling back from training in the UK. It was dire in Odesa, and we still had to get to the hospital.

A friend of Shareef's, who had belonged to the same unit in Ukraine, met us at the station. He drove us to a hotel, a base and a place to dump our kit and bags. At last, we were now able to go and see Shareef. I had been speaking to him for several weeks, so we had already developed a bond.

As part of the rescue, as mentioned, we had sourced a plane for Shareef from Ukraine Air Rescue; we were fortunate enough to have someone offer their services. They would wait for us at Cologne airport, and then when we knew that we were over the Ukrainian border in Poland, they would come and collect us. Hiring a private plane is not cheap. We investigated the possibility of Shareef contributing to the cost of the aircraft, but given his circumstances and how long he had been in Ukraine, that was not an option. ReactAid's priority is not about focusing on the monetary aspect of missions. We aimed to get him out of Ukraine as safely as possible for the much-needed medical treatment he required due to his extensive injuries.

At last, we were finally able to see Shareef in person! What a relief all round! However, of course, rescues are not always plain sailing, and this one certainly wasn't. We were about to leave the hospital when the doctors put a spanner in the works. Because Shareef was a patient in a military hospital, he required official documents permitting him to go. The famous 'blue stamp' on the release papers was missing, so they indicated that discharging him from the hospital was not an option. Naturally, I was confused because we had been discussing the rescue for weeks. It was not as if I had just rocked up and said, "Right, it's time to go."

Frantically, we were on calls to his medical team, the generals and the Foreign Office informing them of our situation. These calls and conversations went on for six or seven hours. There was a growing concern because Odesa was in the middle of a bombardment, and hospitals were often targets. Throughout this time, we were in our body armour.

At one point, Shareef went for a procedure to clean his wound. He was in grave danger of sepsis due to continued infection, and they were doing their utmost to save his arm, which was shredded. Cleaning his wound was a good idea because it would give us a better chance of getting him home safely without too much danger. We would have more time with a freshly cleaned and dressed wound before Craig needed to administer more treatment.

Another complication was Shareef's attitude and commitment to the Ukrainian Army. He had signed a contract and was now working for them. As he had a British passport, he could have quickly just come without making a fuss, but Shareef is not like that. He is a loyal soldier, and in his mind, he didn't want to be seen or thought of as going AWOL or deserting his post.

Throughout our quest at the hospital, none of the staff were hostile towards us; in fact, quite the contrary. They were grateful for what Shareef and our government had done for Ukraine. However, despite these niceties, we were now experiencing a massive problem. Many more desperate phone conversations ensued whilst we devised a plan to get him out of the hospital.

It was about half past four in the afternoon when the doctors and the general told us that the government officials had agreed on the paperwork. They had been in touch with Kyiv and said the paperwork was ready, but it just needed to be stamped.

No sooner did we experience a sense of relief than we next learned that we couldn't leave without a physical copy, and it could take twenty-four hours to three days before it would be ready and released! We knew we could not wait around; we had to go now. The solution presented us with a problematic quandary because we didn't want to leave without the official paperwork, but it seemed like we had no option as we HAD to get Shareef to the rescue plane.

After some consideration, we decided that we had to go. We felt that if we started our journey to Lviv, we would still be in the country, and hopefully, the paperwork would come through. With the green light, we could now leave. Shareef took a bit of persuasion, but eventually agreed.

At that point, Craig took Shareef's X-rays because the hospital in the UK had asked us to get as much medical information as possible so they would be ready for him when he arrived. I rolled them up and put them under my body armour.

Shareef was familiar with getting out of the hospital for respite between operations for his peace of mind and mental health. So with this in mind, we concocted a plan which involved taking Shareef to a hotel for a meal and some R&R. Everyone gave the nod and a wink in agreement because they knew Shareef had to get the treatment he needed in the UK as his prognosis in Ukraine was not good. Although all in agreement, we still understood that the lack of the wretched blue stamp would be a problem for the hospital to give their blessing and send us on our way back to the UK. Everything in Ukraine needed the official blue stamp, or no one was going anywhere, no matter how serious the situation was.

Without this authority, the mission was in jeopardy. The hospital could not guarantee that we would have the stamped documents within twenty-four hours; neither did we have the time to wait. We would have a plane sitting waiting for us across the border. This knowledge was a massive weight on my shoulders. I thought about the cost of getting that flight available and ready for our planned rescue. I must admit that for the first time in ReactAid's history, I was afraid we would not be able to be successful in our salvage mission and it would be a huge let-down and failure. That was not something I was ready to experience. The situation called me to dig deep. Thinking on my feet was becoming the norm as we lived in dangerous times and hazardous circumstances. Risk is our middle name.

Thoughts of another stressful mission flooded my mind. Despite all of the challenges of that particular undertaking, including wing mirrors falling off and failing engines, we managed to make it a success. Digging deep into my resolve, I thought it was time to do the same again on this mission with Shareef.

I asked Shareef if we could have a wheelchair for him. He turned to me and point blankly refused, despite his hand half hanging off, his back full of shrapnel wounds, and his leg and ankle severely damaged when blown up in action. He told me that whatever happened, he would walk out of there, head held high. We had told the doctors and Shareef that we were leaving for some food and R&R. But, of course, we still had to get from Odesa to the Polish border; that was no mean feat.

As I mentioned, Shareef was used to going off the premises for some respite. He was loyal to his colonel, cause and country, whereas Craig and I focused on the mission's medical aspect. We turned to Shareef and emphatically told him that he was coming home with us, no matter what and by any means. We were not there to play soldiers, we had a job, and the focus was getting him back to the UK. He looked at us in confusion.

I was extremely frank, but it was necessary. "You are falling apart, and you've been burst open. Your loyalty is unquestionable, but we must get you to safety quickly. You must return home and get fit; otherwise, forget it!"

You could see the turmoil on Shareef's face as he struggled between saving himself, being considered a deserter, and defending the cause he had committed his life to honour. It was a real struggle for him. You could see his determination and loyalty. If I had put a gun in his hand, he would have been back on the front line laying down his life again. But there was no anger or resentment; the soldier within fuelled him that he would fight for freedom by sacrificing his life in exchange. Witnessing this in a human being is incredible and, at the same time, exceedingly frustrating.

At that moment, we decided that Shareef needed to come out for dinner and hang out with us – it was a plausible move as he was allowed to leave for food and R&R. The arrangement seemed to remove the burden from everyone as Shareef would go under the guise of admitting he would assume full responsibility for himself while he wasn't in the hospital. However, everyone knew the absolute truth about what was happening; I mean, there was not one daft person in the room.

We told Shareef that he would stay the night with us in a hotel, get some R&R, and we would give him some medical treatment to ensure that nothing conflicted with what the hospital had lined up for him. There was much nodding, giving knowing looks, and saying, "Okay, no worries, everything will be good."

On leaving the hospital, we were in an area with no access to non-medical vehicles. Now we were faced with a half-mile walk to the road where we could pick up a taxi to take us to the hotel. Here we were with all our kit, Shareef's gear, and a man who could barely walk. In addition, we were in total darkness due to the bombing. To say it was a challenge is an understatement! The situation was terrible – the weather was still sub-zero, around minus six or seven degrees. Somehow, Shareef managed to hobble along until we got to the part of the road where vehicles travelled up and down.

This part of the story illustrates what kind of people the Ukrainians are. We reached a small booth serving coffee where the stallholder had a generator running. He could see Shareef dressed in military gear and that he was seriously injured. I went up to him and, using Google Translate, began conversing. I explained to him who we were, what we were doing, and that we needed a taxi to get us to the train station. He arranged a taxi for us, and as we had an hour to kill and the train station was about five minutes away, we felt no pressure.

However, the taxi never turned up, and the time passed. It was getting closer and closer to the time for our train. The stallholder was on the phone trying to get us a taxi.

As a last resort, he even started running down the street, asking members of the public if they would take us to the train station.

He found one guy who drove up to the booth in his car. Looking at the size of the car, we wondered how on earth we would get the three of us and all of our luggage in his car. But frankly, at that point, we didn't care; we would find a way of making it work. He got out of his car, took his keys and tried to open the boot… but the boot wouldn't open. After a few minutes, he set about the lock of his car with a screwdriver, trying to open the boot with all his might. No matter what, this guy would get us to the train station on time. This occurrence is a typical story of how the Ukrainians will go the extra mile to help you out, even strangers and in their greatest hour of need.

The taxi turned up as we struggled to get everything into his car. We piled ourselves into the cab, thanking the other guy profusely. Yet again, we found ourselves in a familiar situation, dashing to the train station with only five minutes to go.

You can tell so far that we were not on a straightforward mission and rescue. To complicate matters, we had agreed to support and help Shareef get his girlfriend, Helen, and her son out of Ukraine and safely to the UK. Her route would be commercial as we do not allow able-bodied personnel to travel on the tiny rescue planes. We met Helen and her son at Odesa train station, and she didn't know what was happening. Plans were changing all the time as we had to think on our feet – we now had two extra people to consider. Having additional personnel was a further challenge for the usual ReactAid rescue. We were used to rescuing injured soldiers and civilians, not able-bodied ones. However, we had one goal in mind that was our focus: getting to the plane.

We kept the conversation going with Shareef because we had to keep him calm and in agreement with our plans for as long as possible. Getting to Lviv meant we would now be only a few hundred kilometres from where we needed to be. But because everything had taken so much longer than expected, we made calls requesting to push back the plane by twenty-four hours. We conducted conference calls with the Air Rescue team and the Foreign Office, keeping them updated on what was happening. We were eventually relieved to know that they granted our request, and the plane wasn't leaving Cologne until tomorrow, which was the single window for any delay, the only window of opportunity to get Shareef back to the UK before Christmas.

At that point, we spoke to a film crew and Emma Vardy, a journalist from the BBC, who wanted to capture Shareef's story on film. Craig wanted to focus on Shareef and his medical needs rather than the BBC. However, Emma Vardy was lovely, and while keen to get her story, she understood the situation and was a considerable help rather than a hindrance.

We had some time for Craig to check and change Shareef's cannulas and see to other medical observations.

There was a little bit of time for us to grab some food. Shareef needed nourishment to keep his energy levels as high as possible for as long as possible. We had a long and arduous trip ahead of us.

Finally, we were on the train heading for Lviv, with three cabins; Helen and her son in one, Shareef and Craig in the other, and me in the last one. We were happy that we didn't need to worry about charging our phones as the overnight train had charging portals, and we could also charge our backup battery packs.

It wasn't the most pleasant of journeys. Shareef needed attention every three hours, and the jolting and lurching of the train was testing, as he was in a lot of pain. I couldn't get much sleep because it was disturbed when Shareef needed any medical kit, and I don't think Craig got any sleep. Still, at least we were on our way.

Finally, we arrived in Lviv at about 9 a.m. and headed straight for the hotel. At least we would have some time to catch our breath. I met with the Air Team, who unequivocally requested that we cross the border tonight, and we felt they were asking a bit much. They explained that the plane would not take off from Cologne if Shareef couldn't get across the border for whatever reason, as that would be a wasted journey. So we decided to get a move on and changed plans again as a consequence.

The situation grew tense because the official paperwork still hadn't come through, which meant we had to take a risk.

Meanwhile, Helen and her son requested to go to McDonald's, something we did not have time to do! We could not waste time on unimportant activities and had to get Shareef to his plane! I turned to Shareef and said, "You need to tell Helen we are not here for a jolly time." I understood that her young son wanted a burger from McDonald's, but it wasn't part of the mission. He was so sweet and kept asking if he could carry anything; all he wanted to do was help. We thanked him and assured him he was doing a great job.

Eventually, we arrived at the train station. It was about nine o'clock at night, and I had to ensure we dressed like civilians. We had to ditch the armour, but it was tough. We had our medical kit, Shareef's clothes and kit, and Helen and her son's clothes. Because Helen wasn't aware of our plans, she was asking Shareef for different things, and we knew that none of it was possible. We were trying to get them to sit down and relax. Here we were with these two lovers where passion reigns over everything else, and we were amid a rescue! We hadn't realised we would be in this situation; it was not part of the original remit!

As mentioned, ReactAid's work does not include moving able-bodied personnel around, nor was it deemed part of our tasks. We found ourselves with a problem. If anything were to go wrong, Helen and her son had to look after themselves. I don't mean anything to do with what was going wrong regarding the war, but something more relatable, like getting sick or hurt. We could not divert our attention from our goal. For example, we could not take them to a hotel, because we were on a mission to get Shareef out of Ukraine to the UK. If you get an ambulance, you are picked up and taken from one place directly to the hospital. You do not pick up passengers on the way and drop them off wherever they want. We were in a similar situation.

However, from a humanitarian side, the circumstances juxtaposed with the reality – Helen's life was being turned upside down, leaving Ukraine to go to a foreign land with a man she had recently met. It was not simply her life, but her son's too. The emotions were intensified by the fact that she could barely speak English.

Her situation was very frightening indeed. She found herself in a million pieces, and everything became more alien by the minute as we travelled across the border to relative safety before flying to the UK. It says something about her strength of character: she understood the gravity of the situation and pushed through the challenges.

Eventually, we got on the train to the border. I was on the phone with the Foreign Office, sitting in front of Craig, who was parallel to Shareef. We needed a plan and decided that Craig would interject and start a commotion if anyone came on the train and created a problem for us with Shareef. I would then get on the phone with the Foreign Office and the people in Kyiv.

The tension in the air was palpable; we knew that people were waiting for hours as they sat in offices to receive word that we had crossed the border. This information bore itself into my mind ceaselessly throughout this part of the mission. There was no rest, just hypervigilance. And I have to admit, with all the pressure from the doctors, consultants, military and the 'blue stamps', it crossed my mind, *Have I bitten off more than I can chew?*

Craig and I have a shared understanding, often with no words spoken, as achieving our missions is more than enough. We exemplify teamwork in action, no hierarchy; we all have a job to do and get on with it. ReactAid's strength is found in the professionals working together for a more significant cause than any of us could carry out individually.

We continued our journey, everyone sitting like they were on hot coals when the train stopped in the middle of nowhere. Some officials began carrying out passport checks, and I could see the sweat dripping off everyone's face. There were mainly girls and women checking them so they could mark them with the official stamp that allowed you to cross the border safely.

Two girls approached us, so I went into charm mode, humouring them to distract them and help myself relax in an otherwise tense situation. It was all I could do in the tricky situation, which felt surreal. It was a time to commit to being calm and not give in to fear. The secret is to keep your eye and mind on successfully achieving your mission, no matter what.

We used Shareef's British passport, which was part of the plan, and because he wasn't reported as a deserter or similar, we encountered no real issues. There were a few hold-your-breath moments because they could see how broken Shareef was, and there was no question of why he was getting some rest.

Next, the British government congratulated us and told us what a great job we were doing. Meanwhile, Helen was in an anxious state because her finger was bleeding. Craig looked at her and muttered under his breath, turning away, knowing she would be okay. We had a more pressing patient to worry about, Shareef and all his terrible, life-threatening injuries! We were safe and sound here, but would not be safe until we reached the border.

We were on a mission but did not have official papers with the much-heralded blue stamp. The risk was not yet over. We had made our way to the Polish border, the riskiest part of the journey; however, if we couldn't pass border control into no man's land, they would either arrest us, or we would remain in Ukraine, or even be sent to jail for desertion, and aiding and abetting a deserter.

We were in a catch-22 situation. We HAD to get over the border without the paperwork, or risk losing the opportunity to get Shareef on the plane to the UK. If we didn't make it, the doctors in Odesa had warned us that he would probably lose his arm. Up to now, Shareef had been lucky as the hospital told us that they usually would have amputated it by now because it costs less money and time to send patients home to recuperate. However, because of this rescue mission, they continued doing what they could, with the little they had, to save his arm. Although the hospital had provided us with some painkilling medication, it was not enough, and I had to use my medical pass to buy more from a pharmacy. Fortunately, if you are a medic in Ukraine, you can purchase injectable solid pain medication over the counter, something you cannot do in the UK.

During the uncertainty, there were strong words between Shareef, Craig and myself because it was a now-or-never situation. The tension was palpable. I clarified that if we missed the flight, he would linger in Ukraine, possibly until the end of January, and lose his arm – no question about it. It was a bonus that we had a good relationship, so I would have tête-à-têtes with Shareef leaving Craig as the backup option should we need a firm hand in persuasion. It would be a no-holds-barred type of conversation. Thankfully, we didn't need to go there.

With constant communication with the Foreign Office, we finally concluded that we were under strict instructions to leave Ukraine because the Russians were getting too close for comfort. Their final words were either Shareef goes under his British passport, or stays behind and suffers the consequences. Thank God we could talk sense into him, and he agreed to comply with the plan. However, let us not underestimate the risks involved in what we did, even though we had the most precise plan. We still could be arrested.

So we hatched our Plan B. Should we get stopped at the border and arrested, we agreed that Shareef would say nothing and Craig would do all the talking. I would then call the Foreign Office, who knew the train we were travelling on. They would contact their people in Kyiv, who would subsequently contact the military attaché to ensure that there would not be a diplomatic incident.

The whole situation was fraught and felt surreal, almost like a film. Thankfully, we didn't need our Plan B. Once we passed the Ukrainian border, we entered no man's land and were then at the mercy of the Polish officials to let us through. That could have been a risk but less so than getting past the Ukrainian border. If we had any issues, we could have languished in some cell, waiting for the diplomats to clear the situation.

Another point of consideration was that the BBC was going to film part of our rescue mission, and now we had to think about our timescale and getting to our destination on time. The BBC film crew were so tightly structured and had time schedules to book in slots and had to stick to them, and so much of what was happening was out of our control; remember, we were in a war zone. Someone was in charge of keeping it all organised, and these guys were way more experienced at it than we were. The BBC has reported for years in numerous war zones and disaster areas. But for us, the whole situation was overwhelming and bizarre.

Emma Vardy was the reporter; she was so calm and relaxed, which helped us tremendously. She showed great compassion in her role because she had a job to get the story by hearing, seeing and feeling the situation to create her report. Nothing was fabricated about it, simply a genuine emotion of care and consideration for Shareef. Many BBC journalists and their crew go above and beyond their reporting duties.

As Emma was on the ground, she quickly and efficiently sourced the right people to help us in our hour of need.

Not only did she help organise a taxi for us, but she also managed to find us an apartment, paid for by the BBC, where we could rest and freshen up. There was a slight sigh of relief now as we knew the plane could take off from Cologne and land on the Polish side of the Ukrainian border to pick us up and take us back to the UK. Emma could now carry out her interview with Shareef and spoke to Craig and me.

Emma organised for her driver to take us to the plane the following day. Her generous gesture was an answer to my prayers because the Ukrainian rescue had offered us the use of an ambulance. But when it arrived, the crew looked at Shareef and questioned if we needed it as it looked like he could walk! It turned out that eighteen extremely sick children with cancer had to fly out simultaneously, so they needed all the ambulances they could to transfer these children to safety.

Fighting back the tears, we watched as the rescue plane landed safely. We finally saw the team, the medic and the pilots, Max and Yannick. We had spent weeks working towards this moment, and the rush of emotion was palpable. It was one of those magical moments. We didn't know each other, but we were all united by a common goal to rescue someone they didn't know either. We felt we were all making a difference by doing what we do for the greater good.

The pilots and others, now filled with renewed energy, said, "You made it! I can't believe you finally made it after everything that has happened!"

You must also remember that the rescue occurred in freezing conditions – through three feet of snow, in the bitter cold and depth of winter in Ukraine.

At last, we boarded the plane, where the release of immense pressure created wave after wave of emotion. While Shareef was flying with us on our tiny chartered plane, Helen and her son caught a commercial flight that Shareef's old pal Sonny D had organised. Emma and her cameraman, Barry, accompanied us on our flight.

Considering all that we had just experienced, one thing that seemed odd was the giant smile on my face on the plane. It is the natural joy you feel as a human being when you realise you have accomplished an arduous mission with so many twists and turns. The weight I felt on my shoulders just melted away, and the tension that once revealed itself on my face lifted, thanks to a brilliant team effort.

En route to the UK, we had to stop in Cologne to refuel, and we all disembarked. At this point, I was observing Shareef, who was not looking too good, so we began to worry for him. The stress of the roller coaster he was on was starting to show. We had all of his notes where the consultant had mentioned all the things we would need if X, Y and Z happened. The medical supply coordinator ensured we had the necessary equipment, medicine and additional supplies. I was not the administering medic on the journey; I was the 'get the guts back in' sort of a guy, simply ensuring that we could maintain Shareef in a steady and relatively stable condition until we arrived back on terra firma in the UK when the professionals would take over.

However, Shareef started taking a turn for the worse, and we were worried about him contracting sepsis. We followed our routine, checking his observations, sugar levels, blood pressure, temperature and so on, and he began levelling out, which was a great relief.

Meanwhile, Craig spoke to the police who had boarded the plane with the intent to check for firearms. Craig is an ex-firearms officer, so a conversation ensued about badges and other aspects Craig knows about. He is a great storyteller!

We hadn't realised we would be subject to security checks because we landed in another country. The police asked if we had any firearms or weapons, to which we replied, "No."

Unbeknown to us, Shareef had a large knife tucked in his trousers, and when he pulled it out, we exclaimed, "What the …?!"

"Oh, I forgot I had that on me," came the reply.

Craig and I both replied, "This is not okay!"

Of course, we had to disclose it, so the police came and started questioning Shareef. He told them it was part of his medical kit, to which they replied, "Maybe, but you can't have knives in hand luggage; it is a problem for us!"

The next thing we heard was *beep, beep, beep*. Now we had an even bigger problem! Wide-eyed, we were agape at what they told us next. "We have just detected explosives."

Craig and I turned and exclaimed, "SHAREEF?!"

We explained that he had come from a battle zone, so it's understandable there may be traces of explosive material on his clothing. Accepting our excuse, they told us they faced a lot of paperwork. We now had to figure out what we do next. Then Max, one of the pilots, asked, "Does it make a difference if they are my knives?"

The police officer said, "Well, if they are your knives, as the pilot, it doesn't matter. You are in charge of what happens on your plane."

Without hesitation, Max told the police that they were his knives. With relief in their voices, the police turned and thanked Max and us for sparing them hours of paperwork. We took to our heels and boarded the plane again; now refuelled and with security clearance, we could take off. Finally, in the air, we witnessed some fantastic views.

We were comforted by the quick thinking and kindness of the pilot, and we discussed the situation and how we handled it. Without his input, I knew we would still be in Cologne.

Within a few hours, we landed in Bristol; we were finally back on UK soil! It did seem a bit strange and convoluted as *The Sun* newspaper were ready for us to create the best PR for Shareef. However, this situation was in direct conflict of interest for me and Craig – when you are a medic, you are responsible for safely getting your patient to the hospital. We wanted him to get to hospital quickly and safely.

Eventually, we got a taxi to the hospital, which was a great weight off our shoulders. On arrival, Craig went to get a nurse because we had all our kit, and it seemed easier to wear your armour than it was to carry our equipment and everything else we had with us. The nurse emerged and took one look at us. When we told her there was a wounded soldier outside, she thought we were speaking metaphorically and yet, here, before her eyes, was a real-life injured soldier! She asked us where we came from, and I told her Odesa, Ukraine, and all she could say was, "WOW!" We had travelled non-stop to get here and to this very moment.

There was a sense that it was something out of the blue, but we knew the hospital was aware of Shareef's arrival. The problem was that they had not known the precise time we would arrive. But thankfully, the consultant, specialist and ward were expecting him; he had a bed waiting for him.

Mission accomplished for us; we had rescued Shareef and delivered him safely to the hospital in Bristol. However, with ReactAid, there is always a new mission around the corner!

See page 293 for how you can donate to ReactAid and other organisations mentioned in the book.

PART IV:
WARRIOR QUEENS

Warrior Queens

B efore I finish this book, I must honour the Women of Ukraine.

In today's world, many things are changing. If I were not to dedicate a chapter to women's heroic acts and leadership during the Russian invasion, I would be doing a disservice to my female counterparts.

Ordinary Women

According to military officials, about 50,000 women serve in the Ukrainian armed forces in combat and non-combat roles. Since the Russian invasion of Ukraine, the number of women voluntarily joining the Ukrainian military has surged.

Not only are those women in military roles the backbone of Ukraine, these extraordinary women, no matter their age, refuse to give in to Russian aggression. You have undoubtedly seen many images on the news about these women; the eighty-year-old grandmother staying in her bombed-out house, where the icy rain drips in through the holes in the roof caused by shelling and bullets; the civilian women in their twenties and thirties making Molotov cocktails to keep the Russian troops from advancing.

There is much evidence that illustrates the critical roles women play during wartime. Considering the Second World War, you can see how much the women did when the men went to battle on the front lines. Women became mechanics, farmers and munition workers, adopting and embracing many different roles. Even our late Queen

Elizabeth II, then a 19-year-old princess, joined the Auxiliary Territorial Service (ATS). After joining, she trained as a driver and mechanic with the rank of Second Subaltern.

Eighty years later, women still take up arms and do many jobs as part of the Russian and Ukrainian war effort. Today, with women's equality respected in many countries, taking on men's employment is not so controversial.

I believe that Ukrainian women are the driving force behind the fighting. Many wars are fought and won behind the scenes by unsung heroes, 90% of whom are women. They often do not get the credit they are due for their outstanding work. In my opinion, the role of women in Ukraine is a significant factor towards defeating the Russians.

Women make life more bearable, from those in the hospitals, nurses and engineers who tend to the sick and injured, to the mothers and grandmothers sewing and knitting for the soldiers. These women are proud to look after the men and spend hour after hour making clothing to keep them warm during the cold evenings and deadly winters. In one of the villages we patrolled, I remember one babushka (an older woman or grandmother) knitting a scarf for her grandson. These highly skilled women used their knowledge and resourcefulness to put together a ghillie suit camouflage for the sniper on the front line. These are all handmade, which takes hours and hours of craftsmanship and time.

With regards to the chaos caused by the war, women and children continue as best they can to go about their daily lives, supporting their husbands, fathers and brothers on the front line. In addition, many women are now bearing arms in the fight for freedom and protection of their country. Women are taking control and displaying leadership. They are an inspiration to other men and women around the world. They are dealing with what many men are coping with and still go about their responsibilities as a mother, grandmother and daughter.

I remember meeting an eighty-five-year-old lady who would spend her day baking hundreds of loaves of bread for the soldiers in and around her area. She did it with pride and a sense of purpose every single day. There was no utterance of a word of complaint from this octogenarian. Her focus was to keep the strength of the soldiers up, so she did whatever she could, and that was baking bread for them. Her thoughts were never about her safety, and this bravery was witnessed by many. Under siege, she would risk her life and deliver her loaves to the soldiers.

Maria was another inspiration when it came to the solid patriotic attitude of the Ukrainian women. Maria worked every night at the hostel, feeding and helping the soldiers and police who were patrolling the streets at night. Living in the hostel with my team allowed us to establish great friendships as time passed. We laughed, joked and listened to music while talking about the future of Ukraine. We became very close and enjoyed each other's company.

As the months went by, I could see that her volunteer service each night was not entirely fulfilling her need to do something more for her country. Therefore, I reluctantly suggested that she join the military and put her passion to good use. When she left to join up, little did I know this would affect me immensely. But I knew one loss for me would be an excellent gain for Ukraine. I will never forget those first couple of months. Maria was an inspiration, and I wish her all the luck and hope she has a fantastic future.

Many men have become their country's soldiers but often lack body armour. The caring Ukrainian women used their full resources and drive to find a solution to fix the problem. Some of the women were able to tell me what they had done. They researched stuff online. They looked at expensive Western-made body armour in textile shops and examined how they were made. They got their hands on one and carefully picked it apart, breaking it down to see how to remake the body armour. This new prototype was their modelled product.

Ingeniously, they copied and remade the body armour with whatever sewing machines they could lay their hands on. As a professional soldier, when looking at the finished products, I felt they were as good as, if not better than, the original ones, the real deal! You would think they had come from a professional factory. Amazing – out of necessity breeds invention.

Many of the men were wondering where the body armour came from, and before long, the word spread that their women were making them however they could.

The men were grateful and appreciated these life-saving garments' quality and craftsmanship. Witnessing these women's resilience, compassion and care took me to a new level of respect for these unsung heroes, as I was dumbfounded at the quality and craftsmanship of their products. The making of the body armour came from a much deeper place than most of us dream about. It is a spirit that drives the soul to survive, be innovative, and find solutions to challenges. These women embodied all that and more than the words I can express on these pages.

Ukrainian nurses are like angels. They are always caring for the injured, the sick and the dying. They are helping with up to sixteen daily operations on terrible injuries, traumas and extensive surgeries, with many doing eighteen-hour shifts. They always have a smile on their faces and are genuinely happy to help. Moreover, it is done with love, even though they are exhausted. It just fills you with genuine gratitude. These women are an inspiration to us, to me and to the world.

Vikka's Story

Vikka was our brilliant and brave interpreter. Here is her personal account of her experiences, including some of the time we spent together in Ukraine.

"I remember fondly the day when someone made introductions to a group of people from around the world. There were some guys from Australia and America. I remember meeting Shareef and Tony, who were British and impressed me.

It was good to get more help. We needed as much help as possible, whether civilian or military. They were helping with food and other things when we started a conversation. We hit it off, and I realised we could help each other.

First, I helped them as a translator, mainly because they didn't know where to go or where they could stay. They needed my help in many situations, and it was my way of thanking them for risking their lives to support Ukraine at this difficult time. I fell into the role more and more because I knew I could help those who didn't know what to do in the situation they found themselves in.

Most people think they understand a situation, only to find that reality differs from their first thoughts. People change once they understand. When I first met the group that Shareef was in, it felt like they were tourists. Some were taking photos, and it seemed like they were having fun. After some time, the group split. Shareef and some other guys wanted to be closer to the military, and some wanted to work more with civilians. We had to set some foundations and boundaries, and as I had been working with the medics, our first journey was to go to them.

There was one particular military group that needed support. We travelled to Odesa, and Shareef and his guys taught them many things about the military, including how to use rifles, defend their villages and towns, and keep safe. We did much work with the patrols and defence work in the troops, where I would be the translator in all the lessons.

I am a woman who likes to help and was willing to do anything I could to the best of my ability to help our situation. I am proud of my country, and I felt bad because my country was in a terrible position through no fault of our own. I believed (and still do) that if I could do something – big or small – I should do it.

One way to help, create change and ultimately win is to work together for one cause, one shared goal. Serving my country is an honour, and I am fit and healthy, so

I wanted to work with those who share these values. Being at war was a completely new experience for me and my generation. Working with Shareef as a translator was challenging because I knew little of the military vocabulary. But this opportunity taught me a range of technical terms in English and Ukrainian.

Before the war, I worked for a legal company in the agriculture industry. This new way of living in wartime was utterly different from what I had been used to; I worked in an office and was more indoors than outside. But you must always find the positive in each situation. I was now learning new skills and talents whilst using some of my existing skills.

It is not until your country is at war that you discover how patriotic you are and become. Ukrainians have now become known for our faith, fighting spirit and determination – this is what the rest of the world has learnt about the Ukrainian people. Uniting in adversity is an absolute role model for the world. I'm as passionate about fighting – I don't mean physical battle, but fighting for the cause, justice and all that entails. You soon realise that empathy is needed, and you must be strong.

During the lessons with Shareef and his team, we provided food for everyone – to keep them going and to keep them warm. During one class, I had a strange thought about how to work with a weapon. I thought, *You don't know what is coming tomorrow; maybe you should take the weapon and learn how to do it yourself,* so I did! I learned how to handle and shoot a rifle.

Ukraine had been expecting conflict since the illegal annexing of Crimea in 2014. Somehow we were waiting, waiting, waiting while simultaneously getting on with our lives. It was a terrible time because we were not ready for war. We don't have much medicine for all the various injuries, especially heart problems. We did not have as much government support as we would have liked.

I volunteered in the health sector for six years to help our situation. Humanity is essential; we should do anything to make a difference. We should ask for support from the people of our nation.

We started to change the situation in the system because we didn't have enough doctors with experience. We worked hard to find medicine and get machines such as a VAC (Vacuum-assisted closure), which promotes healing in chronic wounds and burns. And this was before the war! The war has worsened the situation with medicine and medical supplies, so we are grateful for any support we get worldwide.

Being a translator in various hospitals is crucial – I knew I was offering vital skills to help improve our situation. In addition, Shareef trained in multiple medical practices specific to war, using tourniquets, bandaging and dealing with broken limbs. It seemed we were able to help and support each other's work.

Despite the activities involved because of the war, I was still working at my day job! I did not go to the office any more but worked from home to juggle both jobs – this was extremely important for me. Of course, before the war, we had been hit with Covid-19 just like the rest of the world, so I was familiar with working from home for a while. The situation we found ourselves in meant we had already strengthened our resolve and resilience. Getting back up whenever you fall is essential to building momentum and creating the change you want to see in your country and the world. Ukrainian women will do whatever it takes to remain strong; our situation has proved that to the world.

Many women risk their lives by travelling alone to other countries to bring back vehicles necessary to help transport the soldiers and aid workers. They buy SUVs, trucks and buses, and get them back across borders despite the hazardous situations. Like in the Second World War, many women are taking on men's roles and jobs because they are all fighting for our freedom here in Ukraine. Again, we are working together for peace in any way we can. Women endanger their lives daily by taking food, weapons and essential supplies to the front line for the soldiers.

Nothing stops us from being a woman. We continue to do everything we have always done, like look after ourselves by ensuring we look our best. This attitude is crucial when you risk your life to go to the front line with food and other resources the men need. When they see you looking kind, with a smile, it makes them feel at home and gives them hope. They remember the ordinary things about the good Ukrainian life.

We often distribute handmade candles that women and children make for the soldiers. Their dedication and determination are impressive to ensure that the men have what they need, regardless of what it takes to produce it and get it to them safely.

You can see that determination in all our eyes. Women are doing it for ourselves, our children's futures and our country. But you feel it's not a choice. I think it's something inside us now, ingrained in our DNA. Women are now more robust and flexible, like a piece of metal.

When the war started, hundreds of ordinary women made Molotov cocktails to keep their villages and towns safe. For instance, in the city of Dnipro, it was teachers, economists, homemakers and mothers – everyone wanted to get involved to help save their children and their livelihood.

Now that we are over a year into the war, women are taking weapons and understanding the demands of the front line and what they should do. We call them unsung heroes. We call them unsung because you don't hear much about the women. Remember, in the Second World War, women did many demanding jobs such as becoming mechanics and land girls. But our ultimate goal is to have peace, freedom and our beloved country restored to its glory.

Because the men fight on the front line, the women stay home and do what they usually did before the war. They think about the demands on the front line and try to help them in any way they can – army clothing, food and anything else that is required. As Shareef mentions, a woman would make bread and take it to the soldiers daily.

We then met Alison of Third Wave (see her story later). She supported us, providing us with the food we would take to various villages. The first delivery was to the front line, and the people were so grateful to see us with food as they were starving. The food included oil, biscuits, flour, spaghetti, ham, corned beef and fruit – staples. As soon as you eat something, you automatically feel better and stronger, and have a sense of renewal to continue.

The thought that keeps me going is that whatever action I do – be it big or small – will help my people and my country. It's a sort of mini-victory. I feel pretty emotional about it. With victory comes a celebration. Seeing the people you have helped being thankful for everything you do and have done enables you to become stronger and more determined. It's a lovely, warm feeling that you are doing something practical and essential for victory.

There is so much gratitude and thankfulness. We see appreciation as the blood flowing through Ukrainians, and they're grateful for everything, thus strengthening their resolve for continued success.

Even in wartime, I like to keep my nails painted to try and hold onto some of life's 'usual' things – to keep going. But because women have taken on the rules of war, they are becoming more assertive, finding ways to be resourceful, but still making sure they can have new polish on their nails if they wish – making a point.

Our actions reflect the human drive for survival and wanting to live an everyday life where you can go about your business, do as you choose, and keep your daily life as normal as possible. However, life is changing and we will never return to what it was before. Ukraine will be stronger, more resilient and ready to take its place on the world stage. That is my vision – one should always have a dream to strive towards.

What will it mean for us to be Ukrainian? It would be for the rest of the world to truly understand that we are no longer part of the USSR and have not been for many years. We are a sovereign nation with an acute sense of self, our country, our Motherland. We have our own culture and history. We have our dignity.

We must continue studying and valuing education for everyone. This belief is vital for our future, so we won't squander what we have gained. It's about moving forward and not falling back into old habits.

Women make something out of nothing and find ways of doing it. It's called being resourceful and resilient. In Ukrainian, the word for resilient is 'pruzhnyy'.

Dr Alison Thompson – Third Wave

Dr Alison Thompson is from the USA and founded and runs Third Wave Volunteers. She is an incredible woman – a powerhouse of courage and kindness. She has been involved in rescue work for over twenty years – she was at the Twin Towers on 9/11 – and runs refugee camps in war-torn countries.

"I've been doing humanitarian work for twenty-two years. I was in the World Trade Centre on 9/11 when one of the planes flew deliberately into one of the towers. When you find somebody's head on a piece of steel and observe all the other horrors of that day, you develop a way of simply being present at the moment. One minute I can be having a great conversation with you; tomorrow, I might be with a rape victim, and the next, I have Thai food with my girlfriend. I've learned to leave whatever I am doing – be it good or bad – right there at that moment. However, I must add that I have spent years developing this mind strategy; otherwise, I would have gone crazy.

Volunteering runs through my DNA, so it was no surprise that, like Shareef, when I saw the horrors of the Russian invasion of Ukraine unfold on TV, I knew I had to be there to help.

As part of the first few trips in Ukraine, I took both men and women in our transport. We had many orphans and children with special needs, each needing a doctor, nurse and staff who understood them. After a few trips, I concluded that it was better to travel with women. The Third Wave logo is a little heart we wore on our sleeves, enabling us to get through all the borders quickly. We were privileged and could get into cordoned off and private areas, but when we had men on the bus, it meant we were constantly being pulled over and the men were ordered out, questioned and searched. The authorities were so wary, thinking that we harboured spies amongst us.

We met Reef and his men when we arrived in Odesa in the spring. We were looking for somewhere to stay, so we asked if they knew of any place. Fortunately, they agreed, "Oh yeah, we'll take you to our place, which costs $10 a night." Many of the guys were sitting around, but Reef was focused, and you could tell he was a natural leader at that moment. He took charge and ensured we had everything we needed, including food. We cherished the warm welcome and decided to stay in the same building together.

Reef and his men would protect us at our Odesa apartment. He took it extremely seriously when the sirens went off and would lead us underground to sit until the warnings stopped. The other guys chose to sleep through it, but Reef ensured we were safe. Ultimately, we decided not to go underground to the bomb shelters because we didn't want to be buried alive, so we positioned ourselves near the first floor for a quick escape if required.

One night, the missiles flew over our apartment, where Naomi (my Third Wave wing woman) taught yoga to all the foreign soldiers living in our building. We were on the floor all doing yoga together and breathing exercises – with the missiles going overhead! It was surreal!

It was a win-win situation because we could support Reef, and he provided us with much-needed protection. Reef and his men would accompany us on some of the missions giving us security.

We soon found a purpose in participating in the training, which consisted of tactical and medical lessons. We ended up training thousands of soldiers and demonstrating to the combat medics how to save lives, put on a tourniquet to stop the bleeding, and other life-saving tips.

Driving out to secret locations with Reef and his guys became part of our work. All the 'trainees' commented they enjoyed learning new skills in the field, mainly on the rifle range, especially marksmanship, so that we would participate in the drills together. We would ambush them during the practice – I would hide and throw fake grenades at them.

Sometimes I felt sad because I was brilliant at hiding so they could never find me, and I blew them up every time. We would create real-life situations in preparation and readiness for the front line. There was a fisherman and a builder that we blew up at least fourteen times. I thought, *He won't make it on the front line.* A few weeks later, we heard a mine blew him up. That hit home – these Ukrainian men going to the front line were just everyday people we got to know, ordinary citizens who used to run businesses.

A couple of Reef's group were constantly fighting each other, resulting in them leaving and us replacing them with new people. There seemed to be great camaraderie in the beginning, but it became tense over a short period. The issue was that although they were soldiers, there was no hierarchy like a lieutenant colonel or anyone who could whip them into shape. They were all used to just waiting for an order.

Frustration rose within me due to all the bickering and ego-bashing, so I took control and became the leader. We spent a lot of time together and supported the guys for that year. We were paying for their food and accommodation because they had no money. They had good intentions and often said they would raise money, but we didn't see them do so. Despite the situation, we kept supporting them in return for protection.

They would accompany us to some of the front line villages when we were giving out food. There was a lot of training, so sometimes other soldiers and guys would give us protection. By this stage, Shareef's determination and mission was to get to the front lines as he believed he could support the Ukrainian Army.

I found Reef to be open and honest. He would share many personal stories, and it was great fun. During our many conversations, I realised the deep level of his determination and commitment. I believe he gets that from his father, who seems a highly determined man. Reef is charming and kind; you can see his sweet side, especially with the ladies…

I witnessed the good Reef was doing while training hundreds of people; he is excellent in the field. He is an incredible teacher, teaching tactics such as handling weapons and offering other military training. No matter what else was happening around him, he cared for us and was always good. However, being in a very male environment was sometimes hard for me with all their male energy!

Several soldiers were doing humanitarian work, and then there were the mercenaries, two sides to the soldering. Many of the guys were veterans, and they knew about taking risks and combat on the front lines. I'd go as far as to say they were not afraid to die. Some of them found it challenging to fit back into everyday life in America, the UK and Canada after having been in the army. They felt that by volunteering to fight for Ukraine, they would fit back in and they would rediscover their Band of Brothers. Initially, I found it hard to understand, but the more I spent time with these guys, the more I began to appreciate their perspectives.

Regarding the women I met in Ukraine, they genuinely are legends. They are the backbone of communities and are strong. I met a great character in one of the villages – your traditional old granny that every village has worldwide. One lady lived among the rubble and destruction, but when the Russian tanks came through the village, she and her pals took on new personas. I met them all, and the mayor told me that many of them were hiding behind trees, and when the Russian tanks came towards them, they would quickly move to the next tree and hide behind it, hoping not to be discovered. Once the tanks drove past, they would call the Ukraine mayors, telling them the locations of the Russians and offering up vital intelligence. Those old ladies are my heroes.

Despite the destruction, we would still have to go out when the missiles started in our area – usually around noon. We decided that Russians must all sleep in because of the time they would attack! There was one time when we were very close to the enemy. We were about a quarter of a mile down the road so the missiles wouldn't get us, but the artillery easily could.

As I am sure you have seen on the news, many Second World War bomb shelters are all over Ukraine, from all their previous conflicts, so we would go into the bomb shelters to stay safe. Many women had collected beautiful, expensive Persian rugs, lovely items, and meaningful bits and pieces from the apartments that escaped bombardment damage, and they made the most beautiful homes under the ground. In these shelters, there were beds, stoves and even solar panels! These unsung heroes are resourceful and extremely strong. Women were and still are crucial to the war's success.

Since time began, there have been atrocities of war, and this one is no different. I have witnessed rape, abuse and beatings of older women and children by Russian soldiers. I think these are the highly paid mercenaries from other countries, not the young eighteen-year-old Russian boys forced to be on the front lines, often against their will. Many Ukrainians captured these young soldiers and took their uniforms and guns before releasing them to return to Russia. However, the outlook for these youngsters was grim – there were rumours that many who had returned were tortured and even killed. Therefore, significant numbers would turn up again about two hours later, decide to change sides and fight with the Ukrainians instead. They were treated better in the Ukrainian Army than in the Russian one.

Many of these younger Russians had a sneaky way of accessing the internet and telling the truth about what was happening in Ukraine. Whereas in Russia, it is all Russian propaganda; the internet is state-controlled, and many sites shut down, meaning you can only access specific controlled channels which will run with lies and fake news. In addition, the newspapers and media are state-run, so there is no easy way for regular citizens of Russia to get the facts.

While in Ukraine, I met Vikka, who was a volunteer. We got to know each other well while doing humanitarian work. One story that sticks in my mind is when she drove us to a secret location where the Sea Guard hung out.

There was a suspicion that there might have been a spy in that group because when we were leaving, after about ten or fifteen minutes, along the road two huge missiles were launched in the air and appeared to be approaching our car. Vikka was in the vehicle with Shareef, one of my nurses and me. It might not have been intended for us, but it was a bit of a coincidence. I looked at my nurse, and it was extraordinary because she was scared, yet a calm came over me during this seriousness as we looked at each other. The car was driving fast away from the missiles, in case it would lock on to us. It's hard to explain how it felt. It was tense as we watched the missile trail; luckily, one landed in a field about 500 metres away to our left, and the other exploded somewhere beyond that.

When we arrived in Odesa, Shareef and his whole team were being harassed during the first couple of months by the city police. Understandably, tensions were high. The police were now ordinary citizens who had to take on new roles. Everyone believed the city was entrenched with spies, and the suspicion reached Reef and his guys. And remember, although President Zelensky is in power, not everyone is his fan – some people in other cities still support Putin and Russia.

The police kept harassing Shareef and his team, putting them against the wall with guns aimed at their heads, continually asking, "Who are you? What are you doing in Odesa? Where are you from?"

This tense situation revealed Shareef's personality and leadership skills, which saved the day. He was the one that calmed them down and made them trust us.

On one occasion, the police entered our building and took everyone into the same room. There must have been about twenty police officers with machine guns who checked our passports and all the other paperwork and documents required to be in Ukraine. Thanks to Shareef's diplomatic personality and leadership skills, they softened and he became good friends with them all. Quite often, they would all come to have dinner at around 10 p.m. and soon became drinking buddies when they would party all night.

It's important to understand that the police were nervous because they weren't the police at all, as the real police were on the front line as soldiers. The so-called 'police' were others who had stepped up from their various roles. One guy was a senior security official, but in life before the invasion, he was the owner of strip joints! And now he found himself in charge of all the police! Another guy was a baby food salesman. How does that prepare you for this role and responsibility? All ordinary people were thrust into difficult and demanding positions that were not asked for or wished for. It felt like such a bizarre war. I can't even explain it as things would change every few minutes – it was a fluid situation. The characters you met along the way would be hilarious if they weren't so tragic.

❁

Being caught up in a war means learning to see the funny side of life; otherwise, you will go mad.

One day in Odesa, missiles rained overhead, landing in civilian areas. It was no ordinary day – it was Easter Sunday. After being bombed, we found ourselves separated from Reef and the guys. I was with Vikka, and we went over with some of her girls and some of mine to what had been a nightclub. It was huge and had been transformed into an aid station. It felt safe because Russia always tries to bomb hospitals, schools and libraries rather than nightclubs.

We went upstairs, and they told us we must get on the ground quickly. Many women and children crammed themselves into the aid centre. We decided it would be better if everyone went downstairs into the basement. Underground, the corridors were dark. We entered a particularly dark room. It took a few moments for our eyes to adjust to the darkness.

The next thing I hear is one of the women giggling. She tells us to look around and asks, "Do you recognise anything?" We looked around and saw whips, dildos and those bizarre chairs from porn movies where you sit with your legs wide apart in stirrups. We discovered our haven was a sex dungeon!

Our chins dropped to the floor, muffled laughter echoed, and the women's shoulders jiggled up and down. We had children here with us. Eight-year-old Ukrainian kids were sitting on those chairs with their legs in the stirrups, playing little video games on their phones. I couldn't help myself and just laughed my head off. I videoed our new surroundings and took photos because it was the most surreal thing I have ever seen. The bombing of the area continued outside, and a woman, her grandma and her new baby lost their lives during the raid. But down below, we were in a sex dungeon hiding out…

Being in Ukraine and experiencing the front lines with missiles flying around me and artillery dropping all over the place changed how I looked at life. When I returned home to America, I would look up at the sky, see the planes' trails, and think, *Is that a missile?* I'd always look skyward; if I heard fireworks, I'd turn around and wonder what the noise was.

These experiences gave me a small glimpse into the older soldiers' perspectives and what they went through in Iraq, Afghanistan and other combat zones worldwide for nine to ten years.

I now understood why guys like Shareef felt compelled to come out to Ukraine and risk their lives again.

The First Lady

It would be remiss of me if I were not to talk about the bravery and courage of the First Lady of Ukraine. War has a way of bringing the best out in people and illustrating their true colours. Olena is an indomitable woman who has joined in the fight for *Freedom at All Costs* for her country.

My publisher and editor have included this information on Olena as I believe she has had a significant impact on the life of ordinary Ukrainians. The First Lady's intention is to illustrate the resilience of women and children as they face the inhumanity of the Russian invasion of their sovereign land.

The wife of President Volodymyr Zelensky, Olena Zelenska has become an icon of strength, resilience and humanitarian aid since the Russian invasion of Ukraine.

Before she became the First Lady, she was an architect and screenwriter, so nothing would have prepared her for what she and her country have faced in the past eighteen months. Since the invasion, Zelenska has been considered Russia's second target after her husband. Their two children are also high-risk targets.

All her efforts focused on humanitarian aid, especially evacuating children through Eastern Europe and beyond. She has focused on assistance to orphanages, large families and older people who have remained in Ukraine. Her high profile ensures that Ukrainian women and children are often featured in news bulletins and noted by audiences.

In May 2022, Zelenska created the National Program of Mental Health and Psychosocial Support. The program's design is to help Ukrainians overcome the consequences of the traumatic events of the war. Jill Biden, America's First Lady, offered her support by visiting Zelenska on Mother's Day, celebrated in the US and Ukraine, on the second Sunday of May.

When Zelenska visited the United States in July 2022, part of her remit was to address the US Congress. She is the only First Lady of another country to do so. She gave an impassioned plea regarding children and families, and received a standing ovation. This is part of her speech:

"I appeal to all of you on behalf of those who were killed, on behalf of those people who lost their arms and legs, on behalf of those who are still alive and well and those who wait for their families to come back from the front. I'm asking for something, now, I would never want to do it. I am asking for weapons. Weapons that would not be used to wage a war on somebody else's land, but to protect one's home and the right to wake up alive in that home."

—Olena Zelenska

During the trip, Zelenska accepted the Dissident Human Rights Award in Washington DC on behalf of the Ukrainian people.

In July, she hosted the Summit of First Ladies and Gentlemen, dedicated to the post-war reconstruction of Ukraine. Over $6.4 million was raised at the Summit, meaning the Ministry of Health could buy over eighty ambulances desperately needed at the front line and beyond.

In September 2022, the First Lady was invited to Ursula von der Leyen's State of the European Union address, where the EU Commission President paid homage to Zelenska's courage and commitment.

In November 2022, Zelenska addressed the UK Parliament calling for justice in Ukraine and again received a standing ovation.

In January 2023, she addressed the World Economic Forum's Annual Meeting in Davos, Switzerland, where she called for unity and "urged world leaders and business heads to wield their influence in support of Ukraine".

In addition, she presented the Olena Zelenska Foundation to the United Nations Assembly, whose primary goal is "to restore Ukraine's human capital so that every Ukrainian feels physically and mentally healthy, protected, and able to exercise their right to education, work, and build a future in Ukraine." The Foundation has three key areas: medicine, education and humanitarian aid. It wants to invest in reconstructing schools, nurseries and hospital clinics, and provide grants for training and scientific developments.

Zelenska initiated the project 'Books Without Borders', where 260,000 books in Ukrainian were printed for children who had left their homes and found shelter in twenty countries due to Russian aggressions.

The project 'Ukrainian Bookshelf' is being carried out under the patronage of the First Lady. It provides for distributing Ukrainian literature and its translations in the world's leading libraries. More than twenty countries have already joined the initiative.

The *Barrier-Free Handbook* she launched contains a new section with wartime tips and instructions for families with disabilities and the elderly.

The First Lady has won many awards, including the prestigious ShEO Award 2022 in the category 'World Peace' from Polish publication *Wprost* and the Hillary Rodham Clinton Award for exceptional leadership.

Olena Zelenska has been the victim of a smear campaign by the pro-Russian media, but she never gives in or stops what she does on behalf of ALL the women and children in Ukraine. She is an emblem of motherhood, strength, resilience and determination, and is a role model for all women worldwide.

The First Lady of Ukraine Olena Zelenska, supporting one of her passions – the family. Here she is launching a club for responsible fathers, 'TATO-Hub Poltava' at the Museum of the Battle of Poltava in Poltava, Ukraine.

PART V: EPILOGUE

July 2023

I have decided to return to Ukraine to finish off what I started. I am still contracted under the command of the GUR – the Military Defence of Ukraine – and am still committed to fighting for *Freedom at All Costs*.

This time round, I will be helping evacuate people rather than going back onto the front line. I will be going into hot zones and behind enemy lines to evacuate civilians and soldiers like me.

The urge to help people has never gone away – in fact, if anything, my purpose feels even stronger as I know how terrible the conditions are and what a struggle it is for so many.

That Band of Brothers feeling is still there – I am being contacted by ex-military from all over the world who want to get out to Ukraine and help. They too want to make a difference.

I will be part of a large unit run by my old mate Daniel Burke, called Dark Angels. The unit is spilt in two – military which includes tactical training and evacuation/

extract, and humanitarian which includes logistics and aid supply. I am joining the military side.

Helping me and other volunteers prepare to go back out to Ukraine is my old boss, Rob Paxman from Paradigm Security Services. I have also had support from a charity called The Ghost Concept, which raises money to help foreign military volunteers.

Ewen from ReactAid is also returning but this time as an armed combat medic. He told the BBC's correspondent Emma Vardy that it's "about keeping them alive so they can keep doing the jobs they do."

As I said to Emma Vardy, "I'd rather go out and do something and save some lives, and live the life I want to live." My purpose and drive is unswerving and I am focused – to fight for Freedom at all Costs.

Scan the QR code to watch me talk about going back to Ukraine in July 2023.

Scan the QR code to learn more about how I adapt with my reconstructed thumb.

Scan the QR code to view a compilation video of my journey in Ukraine.

APPENDICES

A Soldier's Kit and Equipment

A soldier's kit and equipment weighs around 30 kg. When you go on a mission, there is a lot of juggling with your kit and equipment; your body armour, food and water, rifle and ammunition.

The amount of kit and equipment you take on a mission depends on its duration and type. You have to make a judgement call on how many magazines you'll take, how much spare ammo you'll take, and how much 'link' – the machine gunners ammunition – you will all share. If you're on an in-and-out job, you won't take many magazines and tonnes of spare ammunition. You're going to bring enough for the job.

I've witnessed some guys with little experience carrying way above the required weight. One guy, a tall, lanky kid, was carrying a family-sized bottle of water because he was worried he'd run out... You'd always wonder why he was so exhausted at the beginning of a mission. It wasn't until we opened his backpack that we discovered he had been carrying a massive bottle of water that he'd barely touched. The more water you take, the heavier the kit, and the more you'll drink; it's a Catch-22 situation. However, if you don't carry enough, you go a man down. That means you have another problem.

I usually take a maximum of two to three litres of water. For a two-day mission or, at a push, three days, I would usually drink one litre rapidly, and then the other two were in my CamelBak (hydration pack). I would always make sure I was optimistically hydrated before departing. Three litres is the maximum because when we get out on the ground, you'll hit observation posts where you can refuel if necessary.

Along with your water, you have your food. You take your rations. I like to take multipacks of Snickers which contain three small bars. I can survive daily on these because they're so easy to eat on the move and filled with high calories, peanuts, protein and sugar. I usually take about six triple bars. They suit me, especially when I'm a bit low on sugar. If anyone has glucose issues or diabetes, they come in handy for a quick fix. I always have extras in my kit, just in case. I will take about three ration-pack meals if it's a more extended mission. I'd keep that in my rucksack and one on my belt kit.

The final essential item is your ammunition.

If you are on a night mission, you need your night sights and scopes, so you must always carry spare batteries. You must have your rifle cleaning kit, as your rifle gets covered in mud, rust and dirt. And then you've got any extra ammunition, such as grenades, and any specialist kit you want to carry, such as rocket launchers and your grenade launchers.

It would be best to take your sleeping bag because it gets very cold; however, that takes up the most space in your bag. It would help if you considered whether to take a heavier sleeping bag for warmth or a lighter one for convenience. It depends on how warm you want to be and how much cold you can tolerate! I choose a more generous sleeping bag which makes my kit bag bulky.

So even before you go, you're weighed down with uniform and other bits and pieces. For this reason, I try to travel light. Remember, you have to add your wash kit and toothbrush. It would be best to consider taking minimal weight because you often stand out on the ground for a long time. As each minute passes, your kit increases in weight. However, you are a trained professional soldier, able to assess and understand what you will need depending on experience in cold and hot weather. You learn what it takes to stay out on the ground for two to three days, four days, five days, whatever length of time a mission takes.

In Ukraine, we were lucky because there were soldiers on the ground, and there was kit and equipment sprawled all across the road in overturned trucks, so we were never short of water or ammunition. Coming across previous combats allowed us to pick up shells from abandoned and damaged trucks, such as the Javelins that I mentioned earlier.

Another vital part of the kit is your medical kit. It is usually attached to your belt kit with a tourniquet, and I always carry a spare in my rucksack. Most soldiers take another emergency medical kit for someone else – it's all part of being in a Band of Brothers.

I remember one occasion when one of our crew couldn't find his medical kit when he received an arm injury during an ambush. Instinctively, you pull out your own in those situations as it is usually an emergency. The problem is that when you use your medical kit, you must hope and pray that you don't get hit too! The solution is to know where each other's medical kit is on their belt. Sometimes in the moment's panic, it can be overlooked, leaving you unable to find it. The rule of thumb is to have it on the right-hand side of your belt kit.

Glossary

All-around defence is an encircled defensive fighting position that allows military units to repel attacks from any direction.

To bug out – to retreat rapidly.

Celox™ – brand of trauma treatments which includes advanced bandages that rapidly stop lethal bleeding and dressings designed to seal wounds quickly.

Dead ground – ground hidden due to the shape of the terrain.

EGL – Existing Ground Level. A term used to specify the elevation of the ground at the existing state or current state.

FFD – first field dressings. A highly absorbent dressing pad designed to treat major bleed trauma.

Ghillie suits – camouflage clothing designed to resemble the background environment, such as foliage or snow.

GPMG – general-purpose machine gun

Guardian Bell Grenade – a US-manufactured hand grenade. Note: not customarily used by UK Forces.

Harbour Area – a harbour area is where a group of soldiers will go into a woodland area and set up a boundary in lines.

Hasty Harbour – a hasty harbour is fast and set up in a triangle, so your team faces outwards.

IED – improvised explosive device.

ISTAR EOD - explosive ordnance bomb disposal team.

Javelin – a single man-portable fire-and-forget medium-range antitank weapon system.

Man Away – when an area goes into lockdown.

Man Down – suggests a team member has been wounded and is incapacitated.

Night sight – infra-red goggles that glows in low light and are designed to allow a soldier to find and align their sights in the dark.

NLAWS – Next Generation Light Ant-Tank Weapon, also known as the "ultimate tank killer".

OP – observation point.

Ponchos – a waterproof cape that can act as coat, groundsheet, shelter, blanket, etc.

RIP – Radically Invasive Projectile. Widely considered the most lethal ammunition on the planet.

RPG – rocket-propelled grenades.

SBU – a short form for the Security Service of Ukraine.

Scopes – telescopic sights.

Shamooli – a hand-launched flare used to illuminate areas of darkness to spot and engage the enemy.

SOCOM – Special Operations Command.

Stand-to – a state of readiness.

UGL – underslung grenade launchers.

Vallon – brand of mine and metal detector.

Charities and Organisations

ReactAid
www.reactaid.co.uk

Saving Ukraine
www.savingukraine2022.com

Third Wave
thirdwavevolunteers.com

Ukraine Air Rescue
www.ukraine-air-rescue.de/en

The Ghost Concept
theghostconcept.org

References

The Boy, The Teenager, The Man

childrenlearnwhattheylive.com

www.psychologytoday.com/gb/blog/social-
instincts/202204/how-traumatic-childhood-
experiences-affect-people-in-adulthood

centreforearlychildhood.org/building-a-healthy-brain/

www.ncbi.nlm.nih.gov/books/NBK560487/#

A Cossack From England

www.theguardian.com/world/2022/feb/27/ukraine-
appeals-for-foreign-volunteers-to-join-fight-against-
russia

The Norman Brigade

twitter.com/BrigadeNormande

Call of Duty

www.callofduty.com

James Foley

www.nytimes.com/2018/12/21/arts/design/james-foley-bradley-mccallum.html

jamesfoleyfoundation.org

Front Line

www.dailymail.co.uk/news/article-11376645/British-veteran-shot-multiple-times-blown-artillery-fighting-Ukraine.html

www.mirror.co.uk/news/world-news/brit-army-veteran-shot-ukraine-28379960

www.thesun.co.uk/news/20257981/hero-fighting-ukraine-survives-gunshots-bombing/

www.dailystar.co.uk/news/world-news/brit-squaddie-fighting-ukraine-dubbed-28377094

www.thetimes.co.uk/article/i-shouldnt-be-alive-says-army-veteran-shot-in-ukraine-hrkjrswsh

Band of Brothers

en.wikipedia.org/wiki/Band_of_Brothers_(miniseries)

www.imdb.com/title/tt0185906/?ref_=nv_sr_srsg_0_tt_8_nm_0_q_band%2520of%2520brothers

Dark Angels

www.da-rr.com

BBC Our World, with Emma Vardy

www.bbc.co.uk/iplayer/episode/m001jh60/our-world-brits-in-battle-ukraine

www.ukraine-air-rescue.de/december-20th-2022

Warrior Queens

www.aljazeera.com/news/2022/9/17/meet-the-women-joining-ukraines-military-amid-russias-invasion

The First Lady

en.wikipedia.org/wiki/Olena_Zelenska

www.bbc.co.uk/news/world-europe-63743657

www.washingtonpost.com/politics/2022/07/20/ukraine-olena-zelenska-congress/

Videos

Meet Shareef Amin: www.youtube.com/watch?v=eZBNVWajlmk

Further Reading

Kempton, Beth, *Freedom Seeker: Live More. Worry Less. Do What You Love.*, Hay House, 2017

Thompson, Alison, *The Third Wave: A Volunteer Story*, Bantam Doubleday Dell, 2011

Acknowledgements

I want to thank the following.

In Ukraine:

- ❖   Vikka Krotova, our wonderful interpreter – we could not have done this without her

- ❖   All of Vikka's contacts and friends, especially Alex

- ❖   Alison Thompson of Third Wave – we could not have done this without Alison

- ❖   Maria

- ❖   Sarmat (Andriy Orlov), our Commander

- ❖   Shum (Oleh Shumov), who saved my life

- ❖   Ewen Cameron and Craig Borthwick from ReactAid. I would still be in Ukraine if it were not for ReactAid rescuing me and bringing me back to the UK

❖ Sonny D for his help and support

❖ Rob Paxman from Paradigm Security Services

Ukraine Air Rescue:

❖ The pilots: Yannick Stübe, Maximilian Schmidt

❖ Operations: Kay Wolf, Fiona Knight

The BBC's Emma Vardy and her team

Many kind strangers who restored my faith in humanity

In the UK:

❖ All the NHS staff at Southmead Hospital in Bristol

❖ Chris Pleasance for agreeing to write the foreword of this book

❖ My family: my dad for being there, my mum and my siblings

❖ My publisher Brenda Dempsey and her team – Olivia Eisinger, editorial, and Zara Thatcher, production, typesetting and proofreading. This book would not have happened without them.

Milton Keynes UK
Ingram Content Group UK Ltd.
UKHW010852190923
428965UK00018B/1374